The Safety Car Application & Equipment

By G. M. Woods
Westinghouse Electric & Manufacturing Co.

THE AUTHOR DISCUSSES THE CLASSES OF SERVICE IN WHICH SAFETY CARS HAVE BEEN AND CAN BE USED, THE POSSIBILITIES AND THE LIMITING FEATURES OF OPERATION. THE PROBLEM OF APPLICATION TO A SPECIFIC PROPERTY IS EXPLAINED AND VARIOUS PARTS OF THE ELECTRICAL EQUIPMENT ARE DESCRIBED AND ILLUSTRATED

ALSO FEATURING:

Merchandising Transportation

BY F. G. BUFFE
General Manager The Kansas City Railways

The
SAFETY CAR
GENERAL ELECTRIC COMPANY
SCHENECTADY, NEW YORK.

CONTENTS

THE APPLICATION AND EQUIPMENT OF THE SAFETY CAR

	PAGE
FOREWORD	6

THE APPLICATION OF THE SAFETY CAR

	PAGE
General	7
Operation Under a Variety of Traffic and Climatic Conditions	7
Frequent, Reliable Safety Car Service Creates Traffic	8
Safety Cars Admirably Adapted to Service on Lines Radiating from Rapid Transit Lines	9
Safety Car Capable of Handling Heavy Traffic	10
Track Capacity the Limiting Feature to Safety Car Operation	11
Application To Specific Properties	15
Transportation Data Eessential	15
Equipment Data the Next Consideration	16
Platform Expense	16
Energy Consumption	16
Maintenance	17
Miscellaneous Savings	17
Increase in Receipts	18

ELECTRICAL EQUIPMENT OF THE SAFETY CAR

	PAGE
Lubrication	21
Armature Coils	21
Brush Holders	21
Main Field Coils	21
Commutating Coils	22
Gear Case	22
Axle Collar	22
Axle Dust Shield	22
Commutator Cover	22
Controller	23
Circuit Breaker	23
Trolley Base	23
Grid Resistor	25

MERCHANDISING TRANSPORTATION ... 27

FOREWORD

TRACTION SERVICE

VERY phase of the life of a community is affected by the success or failure of its traction lines in providing a service which is indispensable to the public. Careful regulation, combined with concern for the business stability and the success of traction lines, should prevail in each city of the country. Adequacy of service at the lowest rate compatible with continued efficiency is the paramount consideration from the point of view of the public, and neither factor can be sacrificed to the other without public detriment. Each community is urged to consider the situation of its traction service from these two angles, in order that it may be ascertained whether the increased costs common to all business have been unaccompanied by added revenues sufficient to maintain the service requisite for the industrial and commercial efficiency of the community.

CHAMBER OF COMMERCE OF THE UNITED STATES

APRIL, 1920

General Application of the Safety Car

A DISCUSSION OF THE CLASSES OF SERVICE IN WHICH SAFETY CARS HAVE BEEN AND CAN BE USED WITH AN OUTLINE OF THE POSSIBILITIES OF SUCH SERVICE AND THE LIMITING FEATURES OF THE CAR

DURING the last ten years there has been a general tendency toward lighter weight in street car construction and during the last five or six years street railway operators and manufacturers have directed their attention especially to the development of light weight cars to be operated by one man. Five years ago few individuals could conceive of a car of this type operating in any service other than in small towns or on lines of extremely light traffic in towns of moderate size. The development and general use of the now well known "Safety Devices", along with the shortage of labor and the unfortunate financial condition of most of the railway companies have resulted in the adoption of the Safety Car for a variety of traffic conditions. The Safety Car has been successful because of its own merits, but its widespread adoption has been expedited by the peculiar situation which has existed since its development, and which is largely a result of the war. At the present time there are a few railway operators who feel that the Safety Car is strictly a "small town" vehicle. At the other extreme are those who feel that the Safety Car is the suitable and economically correct car for all surface lines of any city.

The Safety Car is the most nearly universal type of car operating today and actual use has demonstrated its adaptability to a large percentage of the surface lines of the country. However, necessarily it has certain limitations and it is only through a proper recognition of these that the car can be most successfully operated. The average street railway company today recognizes the economies and increased receipts incident to Safety Car operation, and the question is not, "Can we use Safety Cars?", but "How can we use Safety Cars to the best advantage?" Local conditions vary so widely in different cities that no definite rules can be applied. Each problem must be analyzed and the solution derived by a careful study of the chief characteristics of the various lines and the application of the principles demonstrated by Safety Car operation under similar conditions in other cities.

Operation Under a Variety of Traffic and Climatic Conditions

Safety Cars are now operating in all parts of the United States from the smallest town boasting a traction system to the largest cities of the country. The problems arising from the large negro population of the South and those arising from the extreme cold and heavy snows of the North have been solved with equal facility. A study of a number of lines which have been changed to Safety Car operation shows them to be divided into the following general classes:

1. Lightly traveled lines on which the substitution was made on a car for car basis.
2. Lightly traveled lines where materially increased service was furnished.
3. Heavy service lines radiating from rapid transit or main trunk surface lines.
4. Lines paralleling rapid transit lines.
5. Main surface lines.

In the first class are those lines which usually do not pay when cars are operated with two men and which sometimes do not pay even when Safety Cars are substituted. Many of these lines are operated merely to hold a franchise and many Safety Car shuttle lines running through a thinly populated district act as feeders for the main lines, and serve to develop the territory through which they operate. It is usualy undesirable to substitute Safety Cars on a car for car basis especially where large double truck cars were previously operated. The patrons of the railway at first feel that the Safety Car is only a scheme for saving the wages of one man. Its resemblance to the old single-truck cars with the objectionable "teetering" and usually with longitudinal seats, makes the car-riding public feel that such substitution is a step backward, and eventually political capital may be made of the elimination of one of the platform men.

For the preceding reasons it is advisable, when starting Safety Car operation on any property, to choose for the installation lines where the traffic warrants an appreciable increase in service. Just as the Safety Car operators are entitled to a share in the profits in the form of increased wages so are the car riders entitled to increased service. There are, however, many lines now operating with two men on the cars where a substitution of Safety Cars for an equal number of the old cars is the only proper course, and meets with public approval if the railway management

Virginia Railway & Power Co., Petersburg, Va.

has shown its willingness to improve the service on other lines where an increase in service is justified.

Many cases can be cited where railway companies began Safety Car operation on one or more of the busiest lines, furnishing vastly improved service and at the same time or shortly thereafter substituted Safety Cars for old single truck cars on unimportant lines on a car for car basis. This plan has met with universal success.

There have been various instances where car for car substitution was made on practically every line of a property. It cannot be said that the patrons were particularly enthusiastic about the change but they continued to ride the cars and although in some cases the receipts decreased slightly the saving in operating expense was sufficient to change a losing business to an earning one and to enable the company to pay an attractive return on the investment in the Safety Cars. On some lines receipts have been increased from 10 to 20 per cent as the result of a car for car substitution. The reason for the increased patronage is often found in the fact that any new car attracts traffic. The Safety Car in many instances is more comfortable and pleasing than the cars displaced and pilfering of fares by the platform men is very nearly eliminated.

Frequent, Reliable Safety Car Service Creates Traffic

One of the most gratifying features of Safety Car operation is the greatly increased revenue which has resulted from short headways on lines previously regarded as unprofitable. The increase in receipts resulting from more frequent service has always been recognized, but for many years the problem of handling the greatest number of passengers per platform man has resulted in the use of extremely large units running at infrequent intervals. When shorter headways are operated with the large car the increased revenue is counterbalanced by the increased operating expense. When the Safety Car was first used to replace large double truck cars it was necessary almost in every instance to operate at least 50 per cent more mileage in order to handle the traffic properly. While some increase in car riding generally was expected the decrease in operating expense was the chief reason for the adoption of Safety Cars. Actual results of operation showed that in many cases the increase in revenue was greater than the saving in operating expense.

The appreciation of the traffic building qualities of the Safety Car operated on short headways resulted in the second class of application, namely; on lines of light traffic where increased service was furnished. On many lines operating from 15 to 30 minutes headway one could walk from the outskirts of the town to the business district during the interval between cars. The private automobile and the jitney bus flourished under these conditions. When Safety Cars were used to give a 50 per cent increase in service the percentage increase in receipts was in many cases equal to or greater than the percentage increase in car mileage. On one property the service on a line, whose receipts were less than 13 cents per car mile, was increased 47 per cent and the receipts increased 147 per cent or to approximately 21 cents per mile.

The Safety Car makes it more convenient to ride to the business district on the cars than to use an automobile, especially where parking restrictions are enforced. The pedestrian and the jitney rider are both converted by frequent service to car-riders. In addition people who stay at home and shop by 'phone when the car service is poor will ride to their shopping when a superior service is provided.

Brooklyn (N. Y.) City R. R. Service in the Large City

It must not be inferred that an increase in car riding will result whenever and wherever the headway is decreased. A line must first have traffic possibilities or the increased service idea may be carried too far for favorable financial results. For instance, because the headway on any particular line was profitably reduced from 20 minutes to 10 minutes does not indicate that the receipts could be expected to show a similar increase if the headway were further decreased from 10 minutes to 5 minutes. Each line has a limit beyond which it is uneconomical to increase service.

In starting Safety Car operation on lines of light traffic as well as on heavy traffic lines it is better to err on the side of too much service than too little. The attitude of the public toward a railway company is becoming more and more important. The feeling of the public about an innovation is largely a matter of first impression. If the service is actually improved and the public is thoroughly informed of the improvement, the Safety Cars are almost certain to meet with approval. On the other hand if there is no improvement in service, first impressions are apt to be unfavorable and the latitude of further Safety Car application restricted. A certain property substituted Safety Cars for an equal number of large double-truck cars on a light traffic line. During the rush hours the cars were crowded and there was an appreciable decrease in receipts. It became necessary to add more cars to the line, but today the attitude of the public toward the cars in that town is tolerant where in a similar neighboring town where the headway was greatly decreased at the time of installation the car riders are most ardent Safety Car boosters.

Safety Cars Admirably Adapted to Service on Lines Radiating from Rapid Transit Lines

The application of Safety Cars to lines radiating from rapid transit lines or main trunk surface lines has taken place where the cars have been used in

Heavy Traffic Feeder Service in Brooklyn

larger cities. The Safety Cars are admirably adapted to service of this character, especially when they connect with rapid transit lines. The rapid service which can be furnished by subway and elevated lines is rendered doubly desirable when supplemented by frequent, convenient Safety Car operation radiating from the terminal. Heavy loads are picked up at the rapid transit terminals and distributed through subur-

The Connecticut Company, Bridgeport, Conn.

ban districts or to outlying sections where the development does not justify the extension of the rapid transit lines. The speed of rapid transit lines and the "at the door" service of the surface lines are thus combined.

Under these conditions the morning loads are picked up gradually and discharged at one point. In the evening the majority of passengers board the car at one point and leave in small groups. The collection of fares can be simplified by having pre-payment and post-payment areas at the rapid transit terminals. All passengers boarding the car at other points can pay as they leave on inbound trips and as they enter on outbound trips. Street collectors are sometimes used at the heavy loading points. These conditions also lend themselves readily to the recently popular scheme of "Pay As You Enter" on inbound trips and "Pay As You Leave" on outbound trips.

The use of Safety Cars to distribute passengers from main surface lines is a matter regarding which opinion differs widely. In a majority of cities there is a marked dislike to transferring from one car to another. In cases where a transfer will save from 5 to 10 minutes out of 45 the vast majority of passengers prefer to use the through cars rather than suffer the inconvenience of changing from one car to another with the possibility of having a long wait at the transfer point and the probability of being unable to obtain a seat in the car to which the transfer is made. For this reason it is held that where a line operates several miles from A to B and has various branches at B running to C, D, E, etc., that the logical service consists of Safety Cars operating from A through to C, D, and E. The ideal service for each of the branch lines can thus be provided and the overlapping of the lines between A and B with, perhaps, certain additional service will adequately take care of that section.

On the other hand, it is urged that in the larger cities the use of subway or elevated lines in conjunction with the surface lines is resulting in a decrease of the aversion for the transfer and that the patrons of the railway lines are becoming more inclined to take

The Kansas City Rys. Co. Service in Congested Districts

the route which consumes the minimum of time between place of business and home even at the expense of a transfer. It is further maintained that the operation of large cars in trains is the most economical way of transporting passengers over the main section of the line and that Safety Car service should be limited to the sections radiating from the main line. In the majority of cases the all—Safety Car service appears to be more desirable. Certain limiting conditions sometimes exist which seriously handicap the Safety Car operation and render the combination of large cars most easily and economically operated.

The Fresno (Cal.) Traction Co. Service in Residential Districts

Another class of Safety Car service which will be limited to large cities possessing subway or elevated lines is that where surface lines parallel the rapid transit lines. In the case of elevated roads these lines are usually located under the elevated structure. All through passengers use the rapid transit lines and the receipts of the surface lines which formerly were lines of extremely heavy traffic are reduced to the point where operation of two-man cars is unnecessary and unprofitable. To discontinue operation entirely would result in a material loss of revenue because the possible short-haul passengers, rather than use the less convenient rapid transit line, will walk short distances. The use of Safety Cars on short headways generally results not only in the holding of all the old short-haul patronage, but also in creating additional short-haul patronage.

Safety Car Capable of Handling Heavy Traffic

The final class of service is that met on the main surface lines of large cities. The methods of applying Safety Cars to these lines vary in differnt sections of the country, and there is an even greater variation in opinions regarding the practicability of their applica-

Serving Both Colored and White Patrons in Birmingham

tion to this service. The most common use of Safety Cars on main surface lines is where the car mileage is increased from 50 to 100 per cent. The rapid acceleration and retardation of the Safety Car, the smaller number of passengers per car and hence fewer stops, the low floor design, the elimination of signals between conductor and motorman and the better view traffic officers have of the door combine to speed up the movement of individual cars.

The safety provisions of the door and step control and the collection of fares by the car operator tend to increase the duration of stops. As previously mentioned this effect is counteracted in some cases by the use of street collectors and by pre-payment areas. Where the management of the street railway company honestly endeavors to improve the service and the publicity describing and pointing out the advantages of Safety Car service is wisely handled, the people will cooperate by having the exact change ready for fare.

Unfortunately it seems that the larger the city the less willingness there is to assist in this respect. The sale of tickets at a reduced rate, however, often decreases the delay due to making change, In one city 95 per cent of the passengers use tickets.

The congestion arising from the greater number of units also tends to slow up traffic. The congestion is not proportionate to the number of units because of the features which tend to accelerate the movement of the Safety Car, and because of their smaller size. It is certain that a number of Safety Cars can pass over a congested section of city street more rapidly than an equal number of large double-truck cars and still more readily than an equal number of two-car trains. Observations made of congested city service when Safety Cars and double-truck cars operate on the same track shows that the Safety Cars are frequently waiting for a double-truck car to get out of the way and that in the neighborhood of 50 per cent more Safety Cars than double-truck cars can be operated over a given section of track in a given time.

The End of the Line in Brooklyn Residence District

Winter Time Operation in Waltham, Mass.

Before the Safety Car demonstrated its ability to handle city traffic quickly, one-man operation was regarded as inherently slower than two-man operation. However, actual use of the Safety Car showed the factors which tend to increase its speed in their true light.

Track Capacity the Limiting Feature to Safety Car Operation

Track capacity will not be reached over a given line as a whole except in rare instances. In practically every city various car lines overlap in the business district on a few of the principal streets. In other cities the topography is such that there are only a few routes over which every line of the city has to enter the business district and a number of lines operate for a considerable distance on each of these routes. In general, a headway of 30 to 40 seconds for distances up to one mile on surface lines is about the limiting frequency even for Safety Car operation. In this connection it is well to remember that the width of the street, the number of other vehicles using the street and the attitude of traffic police toward facilitating street car movement are becoming more important factors in track capacity. The number of cars per hour is not the only consideration.

On those lines which are so ideally located as to possess no "neck of the bottle" the track capacity of the line as a whole depends also to a certain extent on condition of streets, vehicle traffic, etc. Experience indicates that, with two-man cars of the same seating capacity as Safety Cars and of equally rapid accelerating and braking characteristics, it is difficult to maintain the car spacing and schedule with minimum rush hour headway of one minute. One operator of

Interior Arrangement of the Standard Safety Car

wide experience has expressed the opinion that where the traffic density is equivalent to ten passengers per car mile, when the non-rush headway with double-truck cars is four minutes or lower, it is impracticable to handle the entire service with Safety Cars.

Regular Inspection of Safety Car Equipment in Brooklyn

The Eastern Massachusetts Street Railway Has 200 Safety Cars in Operation

Safety Car Operation by Virginia Railway & Power Co. Has Resulted in Repeat Orders

The Safety Car Occasionally Has to be Shopped but is Easily Handled

Serving One of the Best Residential Districts in New Haven

Safety Car Operation in a Small California City

Congested Service on the Eastern Massachusetts

The Safety Car Solves Traffic Problems in Many New England Cities, Eastern Massachusetts Street Railway

Application of the Safety Car to Specific Properties

CAREFUL AND THOROUGH STUDY OF TRAFFIC CONDITIONS, TRACK SYSTEM, PRESENT EQUIPMENT AND POSSIBLE ECONOMIES SHOULD BE MADE BEFORE SAFETY CARS ARE INSTALLED

ON the majority of the large railway properties the organization is such that reports on proposed Safety Car operation can be prepared by engineers on the property who are thoroughly familiar with the local operating conditions. Many small properties, however, do not have the organization to take care of matters of this kind, regular duties requiring the entire time of those who are fitted for this work. For this reason engineers outside of the organization are frequently called upon to investigate the economies of such innovations. While it is impossible to equal the detail and exactness which results from an every-day association with a railway property, a complete knowledge of the important factors, coupled with frequent conferences with the railway operators, to a large extent overcomes the handicap of lack of intimate personal association with local conditions.

In making a study of a railway property as a whole, a considerable amount of general data is required to give a "bird's-eye view" of the entire property. Bearing in mind that the increase in gross revenue to be anticipated from increased service is of prime importance and that the chief economies are effected in platform labor, power and maintenance, the basic data required for showing the results of Safety Car operation on any particular line are obvious.

Transportation Data Essential

The first thing required in the investigation is a map of the track system indicating all double track and single track sections, and all sidings. The routing of all lines should then be shown on the map. An indication of the kind of territory around the various lines, whether business, industrial, residential, etc., and approximate data on the distribution of population and the riding characteristics are desirable.

The information to be obtained on each line includes: round trip distance; headway, basic and rush hour; running time, basic and rush hour; number of cars, basic and rush hour; regular car hours per day; regular car miles per day; type of car, designated by class number; revenue passengers per year; non-revenue passengers per year; gross income per year; tripper car hours per day; tripper car miles per day; trailer car hours per day; trailer car miles per day.

The transportation department always has very good ideas as to the best lines for Safety Car operation. From the data previously tabulated, and from general observation, a mutual agreement can be reached with the operating officials. The number of cars per hour over certain sections of track can be shown on the map for both rush hour and non-rush hour conditions. Certain lines may require re-routing in order to avoid a particularly crowded section of track, and in most cases where there are single track sections, re-located sidings, or new sidings are required.

It is not necessary to study every line on the system for the initial report, but enough lines should be considered to indicate the results of Safety Car operation in various classes of service. The change to this service usually will be made on only a few lines at first because most companies desire to proceed slowly on any new practice. After the results of operation of the first lines are available, it is relatively easy to determine along what line to proceed with the further use of the car in order to obtain the most satisfactory results.

At least one of the lines picked out for the initial operation should have sufficiently heavy traffic to show the ability of the Safety Car to handle such service and to warrant a material decrease in the headway. At least one of the lines should run through the business district. Lines with extremely heavy peak load riding and lines operating over sections where the track is worked close to its capacity should be avoided. In the South the first lines changed to Safety Car operation should not have an unusually high percentage of colored passengers. In some cases the residence of an important stockholder of the railway company, a local politician, or a labor leader on a certain line may be the final factor in determining the choice of one line over several others. In short, the

THE APPLICATION AND EQUIPMENT OF THE SAFETY CAR

Safety Cars should be so used that the most influential citizens of the town are convinced of their real worth and are enthusiastically in favor of their extended operation.

Rush-Hour Service in New England

Equipment Data the Next Consideration

A complete list of cars is necessary. This list should include the car number, motor type, number of motors, gear ratio, wheel diameter, number of seats, length, and total weight of car and type of brakes.

From the seating capacity, maximum capacity, receipts per car mile, headways and general service observations, the amount of Safety Car service to handle properly any of the lines can be determined. The amount of additional service justified from the

In the Best Shopping Districts are Safety Cars

standpoint of pleasing the public and building traffic cannot be determined by any mathematical calculation, but can be approximated after a study of the results obtained in other cities under similar operating conditions. It is advantageous to increase

the service materially and then if the increased riding does not come up to expectations, quietly reduce the car mileage to the proper amount.

PLATFORM EXPENSE.—In order to calculate

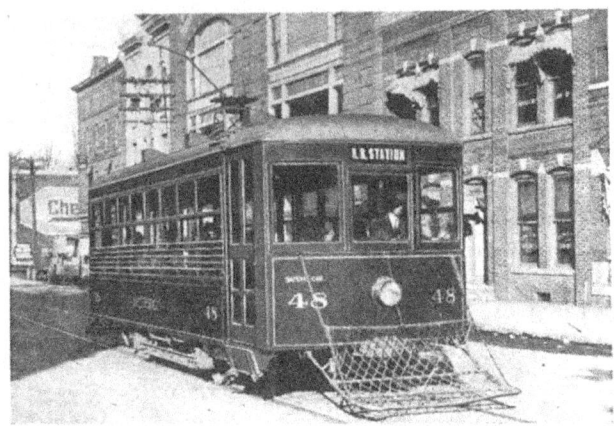

The North Carolina Public Service Company

the saving in platform expense the only data required are the car hours with two-man operation and the proposed car hours with Safety Car operation; the average present wage and proposed Safety Car wage. In general, an increase in wages of 10 per cent for Safety Car operators is recommended. The actual car hours paid for should be checked against the scheduled car hours.

ENERGY CONSUMPTION.—While on most properties the energy consumption and the maintenance cannot be determined for any particular class of car or for any particular line, the regular reports of the company are an indication of the correct amount

The Safety Car in Greensboro's Business District

when the car weight and equipment and the car mileage for each particular class of cars are taken into account.

The energy consumption should be obtained for both Winter and Summer months where heaters are used, for a large part of the additional power used in Winter will be due to the heaters. In the Winter, frictional resistance is higher and the snow on the track and wet rails also increase the energy consumption. From data pertaining to grades, stops and schedule speeds, the energy required for the propulsion of the various cars can be calculated. This will be approximately proportional to the weight of the cars, for while the Safety Car will make fewer stops, due to the greater number of cars and fewer passengers per car, the train resistance in pounds per ton will be higher for the lighter car. From calculations on the energy consumed in propelling the car and the known amount for air compressors, lights and heaters, a very close estimate of the saving due to Safety Cars can be made.

MAINTENANCE.—Many operators believe that

On the Bleak and Barren Coast of Maine

Citizens Traction Company, Oil City, Pa.

Safety Cars have not been in service long enough to obtain reliable maintenance data. Operating results indicate that in Southern climates the cars can be maintained for from 1.0 to 1.25 cents per car mile. Under the more severe conditions of the North the cars can be maintained for not more than 2.0 cents per car mile. Local conditions and maintenance methods vary so widely on different properties that the best plan is to base the Safety Car maintenance on that of the cars in operation on the particular

Safety Cars Ready for Rush-Hour Service

property. The maintenance of the Saftey Car will be approximately one-half that of modern double-truck cars with quadruple equipments. The expense of inspection of Safety Cars will be more than one-half that of the double-truck cars, but that will be counterbalanced by the cost of repairs which will be less than one-half the cost of repairs on the double-truck cars. This estimate taken in conjunction with the maintenance expense of Safety Car operation under similar conditions will result in a reasonably accurate estimate of Safety Car maintenance.

MISCELLANEOUS SAVINGS.—Some decrease

Service for Light Traffic as well as Heavy

in maintenance of way can be expected but sufficient reliable data are not available to justify including this saving in a conservative estimate of the results of Safety Car operation. Some saving in accident expense also will result, but any estimate of this should be omitted. Superintendence and general expenses should remain approximately the same for any given property and need not be included. Since the car miles are increased these expenses in terms of cents per car mile will be decreased in inverse proportion to the car mileage.

INCREASE IN RECEIPTS.—The increased riding to be expected cannot be calculated. The experience of railways operating Safety Cars under a variety of conditions shows that the percentage increase in receipts is equal to at least one-half the percentage increase in car mileage where the cars are properly applied.

The fundamental principles are practically the same regardless of the size of the city. If a certain number of persons ride on the street cars when a certain headway is operated, a shorter headway will not only attract many of those who formerly walked, but will also stimulate additional travel. The percentage increase in receipts for a given increase in service is affected by the former interval between cars, the length of the line, the density of the population and the extent to which short haul traffic was formerly developed.

An example of an analysis of a property and a tabulation of the saving in operating expenses is given on pages 31 and 32 of Westinghouse Electric and Manufacturing Company Special Publication 1614-A.

Safety Car Installations in Connecticut are Increasing

The Safety Car in 1920

More Than 4000 Safety Cars in Use or on Order Oct. 1, 1920

Number of Safety Cars Purchased per year Since Jan. 1, 1916

1916 - - - -	190	Safety Cars
1917 - - - -	280	" "
1918 - - - -	650	" "
1919 - - - -	1620	" "
1920 (Jan. 1 to Sept. 1)	1500	" "

Safety Car in Combined Residential and Business Service, Baltimore, Md.

Electrical Equipment of the Safety Car

A DESCRIPTION OF THE IMPORTANT FEATURES OF THE ELECTRICAL EQUIPMENT ESPECIALLY DESIGNED FOR THE SAFETY CAR

THE entire electrical equipment of the Safety Car has been designed with a view to producing the most reliable and efficient apparatus of the minimum weight consistent with conservative design. The most important part of any car equipment is the motor. The Westinghouse No. 508-A motor has been especially designed for Safety Car service after an analytical study of Safety Car operating conditions and requirements. All of the design details which have contributed to the success of Westinghouse railway motors are embodied in its construction. Among the special features of the No. 508-A are peculiarly effective ventilation, all through-bolts for axle caps, improved protection of commutator and through-bolts. *Oil and Waste Lubrication* is provided for both armature and axle bearings. Separate chambers permit of gauging the oil in the bearings. Large waste pockets are provided.

The *Armature Coils* are of insulated copper ribbon wound with no sharp cross-overs. Each armature coil is hot pressed, dipped and thoroughly baked. The coils are protected at the ends of the slots by U-shaped pieces of insulation. A strip of tin is placed around the periphery of the completely wound armature and over this the steel wire band is wound, while the armature is hot, and then soldered together, forming a solid hoop.

The *Brush Holders* are supported by insulated studs. Heavy, flat coil springs provide the tension while braided shunts carry the current. The spring tension is adjusted by means of a pin passing through one of a number of holes in the casting. The right

No. 508-A Standard Safety Car Motor

bearing from dust and great mechanical strength of all parts.

Particular attention is called to the special details of construction which combine to produce a motor of low maintenance and reliability in service.

The split between the *Axle Caps* and the frame is at such an angle that the weight of the motor is taken off the axle cap bolts. Each axle cap is held by four and left hand brush holders are interchangeable.

Soft steel punchings riveted together between end plates are used for the cores of the *Main Field Coils*. All sharp corners are removed and cushion springs hold the coils firmly in place. Vibration and chafing of the insulation are thus eliminated. The field coils are wound with square copper wire and are thoroughly impregnated.

THE APPLICATION AND EQUIPMENT OF THE SAFETY CAR

Small steel forgings securely bolted to the frame between the main poles form the cores of the *Commutating Coils*. A sheet brass punching is pressed into a groove at the end of the commutating pole, forming a support and protection for the coil. The commutating field coil construction is similar to that of the main field coil.

Sectional View of Bearing Housing

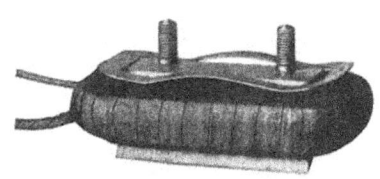

Main Field Coil and Pole Piece

The primary function of the *Gear Case* is to retain the gear lubricant and to keep out foreign material. The pressed steel gear case illustrated serves these ends admirably. It is made of heavy sheet steel of

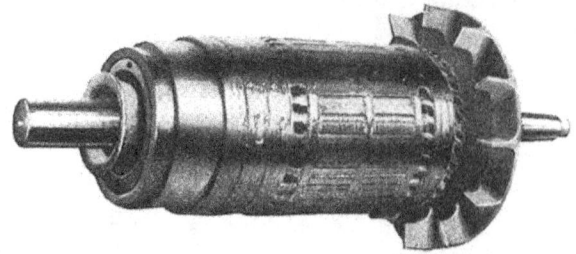

Complete Armature Showing Ventilating Fan

high ductility, bent into shape and amply reinforced at the suspension points. It is provided with a lapped joint along the split to avoid leakage. The two-point suspension gives rigid support and is entirely free from lateral strains.

The improved malleable iron *Axle Collar* and dust guard combination provides a most substantial and effective arrangement. The extension over the commutator end axle bearing prevents entrance of dirt and grit between flanges by centrifugal action when

Partially Wound Armature

Pressed Steel Gear Case

rotating, resulting in increased life of bearings. An *Axle Dust Shield* made of sheet-steel completely encases the axle between the bearings; two windows permit inspection of axle bearings without removing

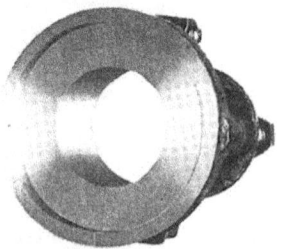

Combined Axle Collar and Dust Guard

the casing. The *Commutator Cover* is made of pressed steel. It is light in weight, unbreakable and easily handled. The cover is held securely in place

THE APPLICATION AND EQUIPMENT OF THE SAFETY CAR

by an effective, yet easily operated latch.

The **K-63-BR** *Controller* is the result of years of development of platform control. Its light weight,

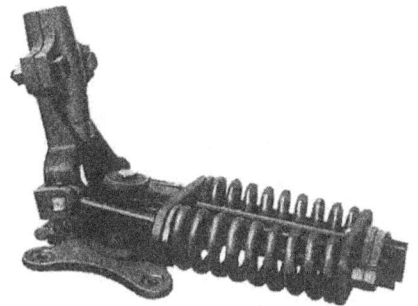

No. 15-C U. S. Trolley Base

small space requirements and ease of manipulation are especially desirable on Safety Cars. The 611-type

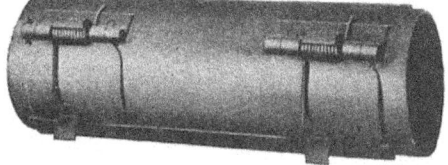

Axle Dust Shield

Circuit Breaker is so arranged that it is tripped and reset by the same handle and is thus readily adapted

Type 611 Circuit Breaker

to use with the *Standard Safety Devices*. It is light and compact and is designed with a particularly effective magnetic blowout.

A detail of car equipment that is seldom given the prominence it deserves is the *Trolley Base*. On cars operated by one man, it is particularly desirable to

Grid Resistor, 5-in., 3-point

have the trolley base and overhead construction so designed and maintained that instances of the trolley

Commutator Cover

leaving the wire are reduced to a minimum. With a 13-foot pole the No. 15-C base easily maintains 20-lb.

Brush Holder

pressure on a trolley wire eight feet above the base. The No. 15-C trolley base complete with 13-foot pole, harp and wheel, weighs only 110 pounds.

THE APPLICATION AND EQUIPMENT OF THE SAFETY CAR

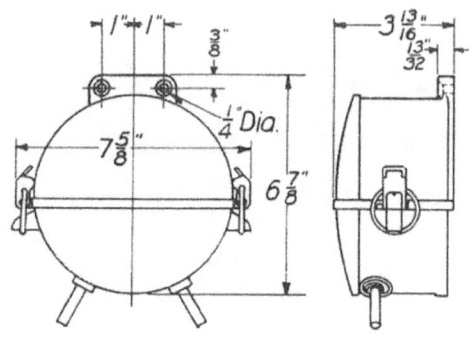

Outline of Type MP Lightning Arrester

Outline of Type 611 Circuit Breaker

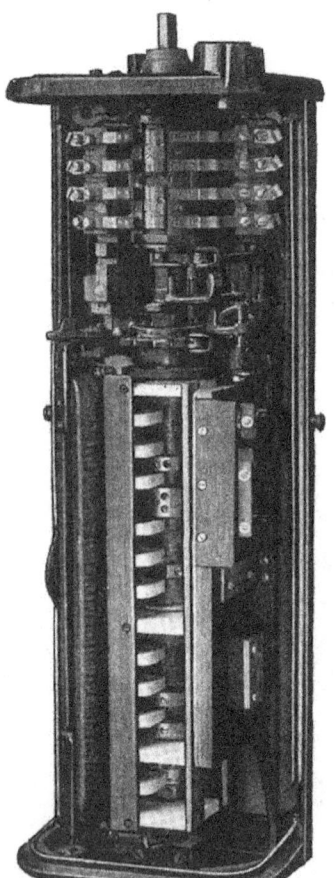

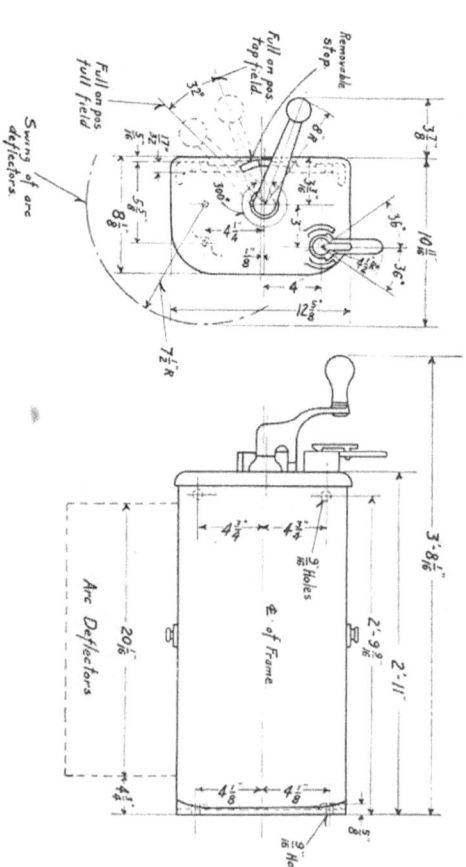

Arc Deflector Closed

Outline

Arc Deflector Open

TYPE K-63 BR CONTROLLER

The Grid Resistor is made up of one frame in which are mounted two rows of 5-inch 3-point grids. Space and weight economy are effected by the single frame arrangement. The individual grids are composed of a cast alloy material resulting in a mechanically strong element of relatively light weight. The grids are assembled on mica-insulated tie rods and are clamped between galvanized sheet steel end frames. The steps of resistance are so proportioned that rapid acceleration is obtained without the jerking, uneven motion which results in wear and tear on the motors, gears and in fact, upon the entire car and equipment.

A complete list of apparatus (including weights) comprising the electrical equipment for Standard double end Safety Cars follows:

Equipment for Standard Double End Safety Car

Apparatus	No. Req'd	Type	Weight
MOTOR ITEMS			
Motors	2	508-A	1700 lb.
Gear cases	2	Sheet steel	
Axle bearings	2	P. E.	
Axle bearings	2	C. E.	
Axle collars	2	M. I.	300 lb.
Gears, Solid Tr. St.	2	74-Tooth	
Pinions, Forged St.	2	13-Tooth	
MAIN CIRCUIT CONTROL ITEMS			
Trolley base with 14 ft. pole	2	No. 15	
Trolley harps	2	No. 25	220 lb.
Trolley wheels	2	No. 40-A	
Lightning arrester	1	M. P.	8 lb.
Circuit breakers	2	611	48 lb.
Controllers	2	K-63-BR	268 lb.
Reverse handle	1	K-63-BR	
Grid resistors	1 set	5 in.-3-pt.	75 lb.
EQUIPMENT DETAILS			
Main cable	695 ft.	7 x 0.0545 in.	90 lb.
Knuckle joint connectors	8	Pivot	1 lb.
LIGHTING DETAILS			
Keyless wall receptacles	20		8 lb.
Mazda lamps	20		1½ lb.
Snap switch	1		½ lb.
Transfer switch	1		½ lb.
Snap switch (D.P.D.T.)	1		½ lb.
Cable	400 ft.	19 x 0.0142 in.	18 lb.
			2748 lb.

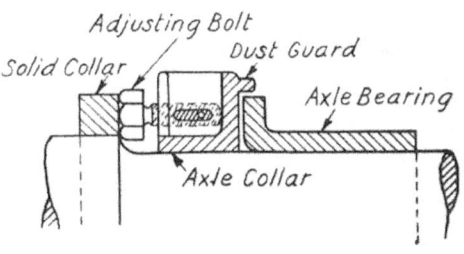

Detail of Axle Collar

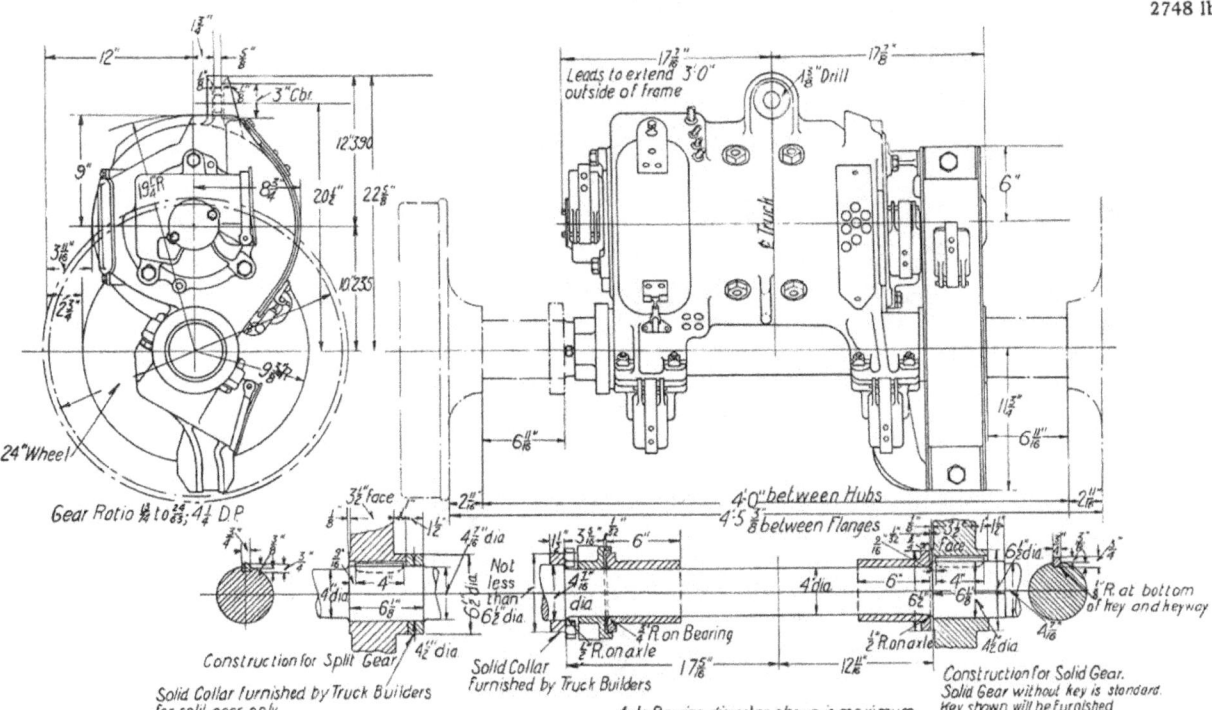

Outline Dimensions of 508-A Motor

Safety Cars Prove Successful on Some of the Heaviest Traffic Routes in Kansas City

Merchandising Transportation*

BY F. G. BUFFE
General Manager The Kansas City Railways Company

PRESENT CONDITIONS HAVE EMPHASIZED THE NECESSITY OF STUDY ALONG THESE LINES—VARIOUS METHODS ARE DISCUSSED, INCLUDING MEANS FOR IMPROVING THE SERVICE, PUBLICITY OF IMPROVEMENTS AND SECURING CO-OPERATION OF TRAINMEN.

One of the subjects assigned by the American Electric Railway Transportation and Traffic Association for committee investigation and discussion at the October convention is "Merchandising Transportation". No doubt if some of the operators who have passed to a region where transportation is unnecessary could return to this convention they would be surprised that the association was seriously discussing this subject. In the old days street railway transportation was provided and the public could take it or walk. Such an idea as attempting to dispose of street car rides by merchandising methods never occurred. As a matter of fact, the necessity for department store methods in transportation business had not arisen. However, "necessity is the mother of invention," and under conditions today in the street railway business, even stronger than necessity, it is a case of self-preservation.

Those of us who in the past three or four years have gone through one nightmare after another, including every trouble to which an industry can be subjected, who have seen surpluses turned into deficits, who have watched receipts vanish in the smoke of gasoline, look back with envy and amazement at the halcyon days when labor was plentiful and wages low; when there were no coal strikes or "flu" epidemics; when our nearest competitor was the "one-horse shay" and when 5 cents could be divided into operating costs, taxes, interest and still leave something for dividends.

The war hastened the industry's arrival at the point

> **MR. KEALY SAYS:**
>
> OME Safety Car operating figures taken from our experiences in Kansas City may be of interest to street railway men elsewhere. In round numbers these figures show that on the more important lines service in car miles has been increased from 26 to 31 per cent, headways have decreased from 30 to 37 per cent, and sixty-six Safety Cars have worked out an actual saving of $425 expenses per day. In other words, through the introduction of Safety Cars service has been very materially increased, headways reduced and the cars have saved in power and platform costs alone approximately $2,000 per year, per car.

where it had to be up early in the morning and stay up late at night to sell what it had to offer. Regardless of the war, however, we had already reached the place where salesmanship methods were necessary. The business is in some respects no longer a monopoly, and while "competition may be the life of trade," it has come mighty close to being the undertaker in the street railway field. As an example, in 1915 and 1916 Kansas City pointed with pride to its ownership of 10,000 or 12,000 automobiles. Today approximately 35,000 of them are in use. Figured at the conservative estimate of two passengers per automobile operated, this means some 70,000 people who are no longer buying their transportation at the old stand. In some cities, to a greater or less extent, the jitneys have hung out their shingle, and where they have done so they are hurting legitimate transportation.

In addition, increased street railway fares have developed another very likely competitor, which is no more or less than the sidewalk. Not that there has been any tightness in money matters evidenced by the people, nor has it appeared that any one desired to economize on street railways rides, or on anything else, yet we have had to face the antagonism and mental stubbornness brought about in many localities by fare increases. Our riders, who very willingly pay double for food, clothing, rent, doctor bills and entertainment, have for so long coupled 5 cents and street car rides together in their minds that our raising the ante called forth a stormy protest which in many cases turned short-haul riders into pedestrians. It is some relief to know that this condition has changed. The 5-cent fetich seems to have passed. The public

*Abstract of paper presented at annual meeting of Missouri Association of Public Utilities, Jefferson City, Mo., June 3, and reprinted from *Electric Railway Journal*, June 19, 1920.

now is beginning to think of rides in terms of service and cost. As a result practically every city in the country with increased fares reports increased riding. Even Boston, where antagonism to a 10-cent fare almost amounted to a boycott, has overcome this feeling. There the riding habit has returned.

The above are some of the very pressing reasons why transportation will have to be merchandised if we are going to sell. The subject offers rather unlimited scope for discussion and ideas. It covers too much territory to do more than suggest some outstanding features in an article of this nature.

The subject naturally divided itself as follows: First, direct methods of selling, which include service, advertising, education of employees, methods of handling and collecting ticket fares, methods of meeting jitney competition and the safety car. Second, indirect methods, such as those dealing with opportunities of awakening public service commissions, chambers of commerce, councils and other civic bodies to the necessity of lending their aid to increase business for the traction property.

Adequate Service the Basis for Success

In the very nature of things, service, in a selling campaign, must come first. The service we give is not only the display of our goods in the show windows, but it is the measure of the quality of the article we sell. We cannot rightfully go to the public for adequate support unless by the same token we give the public adequate service in every sense of the word. The absolute necessity of this is too obvious to require explanation to any operating man. It is true there was a time when some operators thought increasing operating costs must be met by decreased service. That this is a fallacy that will inevitably lead to disaster has been proven time and again. Decreased service spells decreased business in more than a direct ratio. It not only loses business but it loses, too, public confidence. It results in fattening the purses of our competitors at the expense of our own. Our business is such in its very nature that expense cannot be reduced as prices increase. Our whole structure is built upon an adequate, necessary public service, and relief from increased costs must come from increased fares, which principle is of course economically sound and morally right.

There is a tendency for operation to fall into a rut. There is such a thing as obsolete methods establishing themselves by prescription. Examples of this can be seen in the tenacity with which certain routes are maintained and obsolete stop systems continued. Many of us have gone on the theory that because a certain route has become established by usage it must be continued indefinitely regardless of changed conditions. The old theory of a stop at every city block irrespective of the interval between stops is based upon custom and usage. On some lines stops are so spaced that when the time for acceleration and braking has been taken out the car runs at full speed for a few seconds only. Any one driving an automobile knows what this condition means to gears and engine, to say nothing of the loss in time. Therefore, our wares must in any case be better displayed and better adapted to the needs of the public by revision in routes and stops. Especially are changes necessary in congested districts.

Scientific Traffic Study Made

For example, in Kansas City we have for some months enjoyed the services of John A. Beeler, consulting engineer of New York City. Mr. Beeler has acquired a most enviable reputation in the United States in straightening out traffic tangles. His work in Washington during the war, in Boston and in Philadelphia speaks for itself. Very recently Mr. Beeler has been retained by the Public Service Corporation of New Jersey and the Chicago Surface Lines. Through a rearrangement of stops in the downtown district, by the use of the double berthing system and loading platforms, Mr. Beeler has been able to secure on many lines an increase in speed of more than 100 per cent. On one important street, in a block where formerly sixty cars an hour passed in one direction, we are now able to put through ninety-three. The effect of this is of course most significant. It means that those cars scheduled to hit the downtown district at the beginning of the rush hour are there on time when they will do the most good. Due to Mr. Beeler's rearrangement, we now find it possible to maintain our system speed at more than 9 m.p.h., and of course increased schedule speed and regular headways mean just as large an increase in service as the addition of more cars. In fact, it is more, because additional cars, if not at the right place when needed, serve no useful purpose.

I think therefore every one will admit that in merchandising transportation the first essential is to see that service is all modern operating methods can make it. Service, after all, starts in the carhouses. Clean, well maintained, well painted cars are our biggest advertisement. Very often an entire system is judged by the apperance of its cars on the street, and too much attention cannot be paid to this phase of operation. A policy of retrenchment that starts with the equipment will end in disaster if continued.

Let the People Know

Service being the first step in selling car rides, it very naturally follows that keeping the public informed of this service should be the next. There is no more practical reason for a street railway company "hiding its light under a bushel" than there is for a department store. The public is very appreciative of the printed word. The repeated suggestion that your city has the best street railway service in the country, if in any way at all backed up by facts, will very shortly meet a receptive mood in the public mind. Local pride in one's city will help bring about this mental condition. People can be educated to point proudly to their street railway service the same as to their public buildings and parks.

Advertising from the standpoint of selling transportation is a different problem than that presented by the good will and public policy advertising campaigns which have been carried on so extensively in the past five years by public service companies. A most excellent medium is the space provided by the car itself. Perhaps there is no more effective advertising than dash cards. A hanging frame on the inside from the car roof is also most desirable space. A notable example of this is furnished in Philadelphia, and each week sees a different message on Philadelphia's service in the frames. The New York Interborough uses the space on the two front windows of each car, and under the title of the "Subway Sun" communicates new data to the car riding public each week.

This direct advertising should enlarge on service changes, and copy for it should be worked out with the sole purpose of directing the attention of the rider to facilities offered by the street railway system and service given. One good feature which can be emphasized is the cost of operating an automobile. It has been demonstrated that no type of car, not even the smallest, can be operated for less than 10 cents a mile. In the larger cities to drive an automobile downtown to business and back costs from 75 cents to $1.50 a day. Another strong feature which can be utilized is the fact that the street railway system in any community is essential, that upon it the community's growth has been predicated and that system and service have both been outlined on the basis of handling all the people in the community all the time. This being the case, it is to the interest of every citizen to see that the local car line is supported, that jitney competition is not allowed and that a full measure of co-operation be given by the public. Under our present service-at-cost franchises (and in those states which have utility commissions practically all franchises resolve themselves into this type) the rate of fare depends very directly upon the amount of riding. There can be no hope for decreased fares unless the volume of riding increases and service is utilized to the fullest extent.

The moving picture theater offers a very productive field for the advertising man. Few people who ride the cars have any conception of the machinery back of their daily ride. They have but a limited knowledge of shops, power plant, carhouses, regular inspection force, track department and other branches of the organization that produces city transportation. These things can be filmed and will serve to educate the public in the rudimentary elements of its transportation.

Education of Trainmen Important

Another essential point in selling transportation is proper education of the salesman himself. Trainmen are the company's representatives, and too often their training involves only operation of cars and not stimulation of business. I believe the greatest field ahead of street railway operators today lies in the training of transportation forces, and at the wages today being paid there is no good reason why we cannot secure the service of men's heads as well as their hands.

Such training involves courtesy, politeness, careful operation, and goes even deeper. We must first make trainmen realize that in a sense they are salesmen, that they are responsible for much more than the ordinary operation of cars. We must bring them to a realization of the importance of their own position. We must awaken in them a higher sense of their responsibility. This means education, and, like most things worth having, will take time and unceasing patience to secure. It starts at the employment office, where greater endeavor must be made to secure a higher type of employee. It means more intensive schooling and instruction. Frequent meetings of employees and talks by officials of the company help. A company publication is another good method. In Kansas City, through published articles and talks to the men, we have endeavored to get them all interested in the company's financial statement, which shows the result of their own operation. These statements, in easily understood terms, are published in the employee's magazine every month. Every wage increase we have made in the past sixteen months has been based upon such financial statements. We have succeeded in a large measure in this policy, and I believe today employees of The Kansas City Railways are better informed as to the company's financial position and its policies than is general throughout the country in traction systems.

Just last week more than 3,100 employees signed petitions addressed to the City Council demanding that jitneys be driven off the streets. In several divisions there were not to exceed a dozen employees who refused to sign the petitions. The employees themselves requested that these men be discharged.

The active interest and co-operation of the employees of any company is a most vital factor in the sale of street car rides. Although there are many other reasons why Philadelphia has been able to succeed without fare increases, the biggest factor in the success of that company has been the co-operation of its 10,000 men. This co-operation has not been the result of a month's work or a year's work, but has been secured by constant hammering along the same lines for the past seven or eight years.

THE SAFETY CAR

THE safety car was first operated in 1916 and met with immediate success. On account of its small size and its one-man operation, it was regarded for a time, by the majority of operators, as suitable for only lightly traveled lines in small cities. It had a certain physical resemblance to the single-truck "dinkeys" of unpleasant memory. One-man operation began in horse-car days and had been gradually abandoned partly because of objections of the platform men, and partly because the use of only one man on existing cars resulted in slow schedules and generally unsatisfactory service. The modern safety car, however, eliminates all of these objections.

The standard safety car is approximately 28 feet in length and 7 feet 10 inches in width. The double-end car seats 32 persons and the single-end car seats 35 persons. The weight of the car completely equipped but without passenger load is 16,000 pounds. Twenty-four or 26 in. wheels are used on practically all cars.

The safety features which are included on the standard car are of primary importance. They actually do prevent accidents and they also are of material assistance in winning over the public when safety cars are first used in any particular town, and they contribute by labor saving to the speed of operation. With the usual safety devices it is necessary for the brakes to be applied, bringing the car to a stop before the door can be opened. Likewise, the door must be closed before the brakes can be released and the car started. In case the operator releases the handle of the controller through illness or inattention or for any other cause, the power is immediately cut off, the brakes applied, the track sanded and the doors released so that they can readily be opened by hand. Boarding and alighting accidents have been almost eliminated by the safety features and there has been a number of instances where the emergency features have been brought into action and accidents averted which otherwise would have occurred.

In view of the variety of designs of older cars and the diversity of opinions regarding almost every detail of their construction, it is not surprising that there have been various modifications of safety cars constructed for various conditions of service. Rather, it is surprising that so few changes have been made, and that essentially the same car has been found adequate to meet the variety of service in which standard safety cars are used. As a result of standardization, there is undoubtedly considerable advantage in first cost and in quickness of obtaining renewal parts.

In certain cities, where physical limitations permit, wider aisles and a greater distance between seats are desirable. In some cities, loading conditions are such that double doors are considered essential. In others, the seating arrangement is changed to provide longitudinal seats on one side of the car for a short length at the front end of a single-end car or at both ends where double-end cars are used. There has been a general tendency in the northern part of this country and in Canada to strengthen various parts of the car and to protect the interior of the car better from cold. Where cars are heavier than normal and where severe snow or grade conditions are encountered, two 35 hp. motors may be required instead of the customary 25 hp. motors. When double doors are used, provision should be made for operating each door independently of the other.

The use of safety cars has resulted in the expected decrease in operating expenses. The principal item in street railway operating expense is wages of conductors and motormen. In order to share the benefits of safety car operation with the car operator, it is customary to increase his rate of pay 10 per cent above that of a conductor or motorman on two-man cars. There is thus a saving in platform labor per car mile of 45 per cent.

The safety car effects savings in maintenance of cars and equipment. On account of its light weight, repairs are easily made and renewal parts cost less. As compared with double-truck cars, there are fewer and lighter parts to maintain; and as compared with older single-truck cars, the same weight economies obtain while the improved design of truck and body eliminates many of the strains set up by the rocking prevalent in the older cars. The actual main-

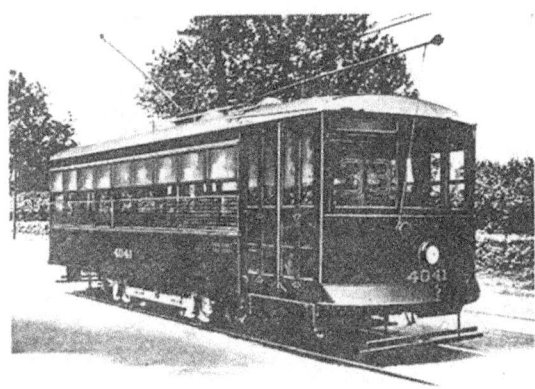

The United Railways & Electric Company, Baltimore, is One of the Largest Operators of Safety Cars

tenance of safety cars depends largely on local conditions, but usually will be between 1.5 and 2.0 cents per car mile. On a number of properties, safety car maintenance has been found to be 40 to 50 per cent of that of the average double-truck car, on a mileage basis.

Maintenance of track and roadway will undoubtedly be decreased by safety car operation. The exact amount saved is doubtful on account of the difficulty of segregating maintenance for any particular sections of track or conditions of operation. When new track is laid or old track is rebuilt, there should be a very material saving, for less expensive construction may be used with light-weight safety cars than with heavy double-truck cars.

Energy consumption varies approximately as the ton-mileage and hence the saving per car mile will be almost directly proportional to the saving in car weight. As compared with heavier equipment, the less power drawn by the safety car results in less line drop with resulting higher voltage at the car and higher efficiency of distribution. When generating and converting equipment are loaded to capacity, safety car operation may make it possible to postpone the purchase of additional power house and substation equipment. When safety cars are used in new installations, a lower investment is necessary for complete generating, conversion and distribution systems than when heavy cars are operated.

While the safety car was first proposed as a means of reducing operating expense in com-

Safety Car of the San Francisco-Oakland Terminal Railways

SAFETY CAR OPERATION

	Present Operation	Proposed Operation
Car Type	Double Truck	Safety
Weight of car with av. load, tons	18.65	9.25
Seating capacity	40	32
Number of motors per car	2	2
Type of motor	No. 532-B	No. 508-A
Round trip distance, miles	10.32	10.32
Round trip time, including layover:		
Non-rush service, minutes	60	60
Rush service, minutes	64	60
Normal headway, non-rush, min.	10	6
Maximum number of cars, non-rush	6	10
Normal headway, rush, minutes	5	3
Maximum number of cars, rush	12	20
Total car hours per day	150	260
Total car miles per day	1505	2680
Kw. hrs. per car mile at sub-station	2.73	1.255
Power cost per day, 1.25c per kw. hr.	$ 51.40	$ 42.00
Labor cost per day, 47c per man-hour	141.10	
Labor cost per day, 52c per man-hour		135.10
Car maintenance per day, 2.98c per car mile	44.90	
Car maintenance per day, 1.5c per car mile		40.20
Total cost of power, labor and maintenance per day	$ 237.40	$ 217.30
Total cost of power, labor and maintenance per year	$86650.00	$ 79315.00
Saving in operating expenses per year		$ 7335.00
Increase in car mileage with safety cars		78%
Estimated increase in earnings		39%
Estimated increase in annual earnings, 39% of $169215		$ 65995.00
Total increase in net annual revenue		73330.00
Cost of 22 new cars, $6000 each		132000.00
Return on investment		55.5%

bating jitney bus competition in the West and Northwest, shorter headways were operated and it was found that the increase in receipts due to the improved service outweighed the reduction in operating expense. In the last five years it has been demonstrated frequently that the most successful safety car applications from the standpoint of financial return and popular favor, are those where the service is considerably increased. The result has been that although the original applications were on the basis of not more than 25 per cent increase in service, the later applications which have been most successful have been made on the basis of 50 to 100 per cent increase in service.

The 1920 report of the American Electric Railway Association, Committee on Safety Car Operation, says of earnings: "The averages of the companies which increased their schedules with safety cars show an average of 40.5 per cent increase in safety car mileage compared to former two-man car mileage on the lines affected, with a corresponding decrease in the car mile gross earnings of but 0.93 per cent. That is, the gross earnings with safety cars show substantially the same percentage of increase as the car miles operated."

The following table shows the present and proposed service and the results to be obtained by replacing double-truck cars on a base headway of 10 minutes with safety cars on a base headway of 6 minutes.

United Railways & Electric Company Baltimore

The United Railways & Electric Company of Baltimore is one of the larger operators of safety cars in congested districts. The original installation on the Fremont Line was made in July, 1920 with 33 cars. The Fremont Line skirts the congested section of the city, and crosses a comparatively large number of the traction lines. Heavy transfer service results. Actual operation during a period of several years has fully demonstrated the ability of this type of transportation to meet most exacting conditions.

The car employed is 30 feet long and is provided with a wide aisle. A longitudinal seat is placed at each corner of the car to provide more standing room, and also to afford the least possible resistance to ingress and egress of passengers who are mostly short distance riders.

Los Angeles

Safety car operation was initiated in Los Angeles, in July, 1920. The first line was a shuttle which served an outlying section of the city and connected two lines running to the principal business district. The second line connects a number of main lines and provides a cross-town service outside the business district. Operation of safety cars was started in the business district in August, 1921. Greatly improved service was furnished, twelve safety cars superseding nine older cars of the same seating capacity.

Brooklyn Rapid Transit Company

One large company, the Brooklyn Rapid Transit Company, uses safety cars extensively for heavy traffic feeders and for congested city service in Brooklyn. Their successful operation is an example of the usefulness of this type of car in a large city. Other examples of the extensive use of safety cars are the Eastern Massachusetts Street Railway Company and the Stone & Webster Corporation. These companies have hundreds of safety cars in service in various towns served by their systems, where in many cases safety cars are operating in congested traffic. The original safety cars met these requirements so satisfactorily and with such marked improvement in service that large numbers of safety cars are being added by these two companies from time to time.

Pennsylvania-Ohio Electric Company

The Pennsylvania-Ohio Electric Company operates safety cars in Sharon, New Castle and

Safety Cars are Operated by the Fresno Traction Company

Youngstown, all of which cities are busy industrial centers. Safety car operation was started in September, 1919. On the initial installation the number of seats furnished was increased 84 per cent by providing a six-minute service instead of ten-minute service. Safety cars were used on other lines in rapid succession with the most gratifying results. On lines where the service remained the same, riding decreased during the recent industrial depression; but on the safety car lines receipts increased very materially.

Mr. Clinton D. Smith, general superintendent of the company, summarizes the features of the safety car which contribute to the merchandising of transportation as follows:

"(1) The economical operation of the car permits more frequent headway.

"(2) The car, being the last word in modern mechanical electrical equipment, appeals to the people in the same manner as the modern department store, and encourages its frequent use.

"(3) Appreciation of the fact that the car is fully equipped with safety devices tends to increase the number of rides per capita.

"(4) Finally, our analysis indicates conclusively that there are fewer accidents with the safety cars, as compared with two-man cars. There has been a practical elimination of boarding and alighting accidents."

Safety Car of the Union Traction Company of Santa Cruz

*The Safety Car in Congested Service
Kansas City Railways*

EQUIPMENT FOR STANDARD DOUBLE-END SAFETY CAR
Two 25 hp. Motors

Motor Items:

Apparatus	No. Req'd	Type	Weight Pounds
Motors	2	508-A	
Gear cases	2	Pressed steel	
Axle bearings	2	Pinion end	
Axle bearings	2	Comm. end	2100
Axle collars	2	M.I.	
Gears, solid tr. st.	2	74-tooth	
Pinions, forged st.	2	13-tooth	

Main Circuit Control Items:

Trolley base with 14-ft. pole	2	No. 15	.....
Trolley harps	2	No. 25	220
Trolley wheels	2	No. 40-A	.....
Lightning arrester	1	M.P.	8
Circuit breakers	2	611	48
Controllers	2	K-63-BR	268
Reverse handle	1	K-63-BR	.....
Grid resistors	1 set	5 in. 3 pt.	75

Equipment Details:

Main cable	695 ft.	7x".064	90
Knuckle joint connectors	8	Pivot	1

Lighting Details:

Keyless wall receptacles	20	....	
Mazda lamps	20	....	
Snap switch	1	....	29
Transfer switch	1	....	
Snap switch (d.p.d.t.)	1	....	
Cable	400 ft.	19x".0142	

Total: 2839

For Single-End Operation—Omit:
1 Trolley   165 Ft. Main cable 7x".0545
1 Controller   1—D.P.D.T. snap switch
1 Circuit breaker   1—Transfer switch

EQUIPMENT FOR DOUBLE-END SAFETY CAR
Two 35 hp. Motors

Motor Items:

Apparatus	No. Req'd	Type	Weight Pounds
Motors	2	510	
Gear cases	2	Pressed steel	
Axle bearings	2	Pinion end	
Axle bearings	2	Comm. end	2985
Axle collars	2	M.I.	
Gears, solid tr. st.	2	69-tooth	
Pinions, forged st.	2	13-tooth	

Main Circuit Control Items:

Trolley base with 14-ft. pole	2	No. 15	.....
Trolley harps	2	No. 25	220
Trolley wheels	2	No. 40-A	.....
Lightning arrester	1	M.P.	8
Circuit breakers	2	611	48
Controllers	2	K-63-BR	268
Reverse handle	1	K-63-BR	.....
Grid resistors	1 Set	5 in. 3 pt.	113

Equipment Details:

Main cable	695 ft.	7x".064	111
Knuckle joint connectors	8	Pivot	1

Lighting Details:

Keyless wall receptacles	20	....	
Mazda lamps	20	....	
Snap switch	1	....	29
Transfer switch	1	....	
Snap switch (d.p.d.t.)	1	....	
Cable	400 ft.	19x".0142	

Total: 3693

For Single-End Operation—Omit:
1 Trolley   165 ft. main cable 7x".064
1 Controller   1—D.P.D.T. snap switch
1 Circuit breaker   1—Transfer switch

For magnetic line switch, omit circuit breakers and add the following:

FOR DOUBLE-END:

Control switch with fuses	2	494-C	14
Line switch	1	801-E	95
Insulating bolts	4	....	6
Ratchet switches for:			
Controller	2		15
Control cable	150 ft.	19x".0142	5

FOR SINGLE-END:

Control switch with fuses	1	494-C	7
Line switch	1	801-E	96
Insulating bolts	4	....	6
Ratchet switch for:			
Controller	1		7½
Control cable	100 ft.		3½

A Safety Car of the Pacific Electric Railway

THE SAFETY CAR

A FEW OF THE 66 SAFETY CARS OPERATED IN TERRE HAUTE, IND.

During the past few years the electric railways of the country have been confronted with rapidly increasing cost of operation while their gross income has remained practically unchanged. A vast amount of study and attention has been given by the engineering and financial interests to assist the railways in the continuance of business under the existing unfavorable conditions.

The most encouraging results achieved by these studies have been the development and the many successful installations of the one-man light weight Safety Car. Examples of what may be accomplished by this radical departure from the ordinary method of street railway transportation may be found in almost every section of the United States. Briefly stated the reasons for the success of this innovation are the following:

1. Improvement in service.
2. Freedom from accidents.
3. Increase in riding habit.
4. Lower maintenance cost.
5. Reduction in labor cost.
6. Reduction in power consumption.

As a result of these features, the operating company's net income has shown a marked improvement in almost every case. This increase in gross receipts combined with the marked reduction in cost of operation effects sufficient saving to insure profitable operation on roads previously run at a loss.

Report of A. E. R. A. Committee

The conclusions of the committee on one-man car operation presented to the American Electric Railway Association in October, 1919, present the findings of a competent body of operating men on this subject:

1. The Safety Car is one of the most important improvements in street railway service that has appeared for many years. Its valuable features in the order of their importance are:
   (a) Greatly improved service to the public, both as to frequency and safety.
   (b) Increased earnings for the company.
   (c) Decreased operating expenses.
2. One-man operation alone, while useful in saving platform expense in the smaller communities, is not comparable with the improved service that can be obtained with the Light Weight Safety Car with its more frequent headway and greater average speed.

106 SAFETY CARS ON THE BROOKLYN RAPID TRANSIT SYSTEM EQUIPPED WITH GE-264 MOTORS AND K-63 CONTROL

3. The savings obtainable from one-man cars should be shared with the trainmen in the form of a higher hourly rate for the operators of such cars than is paid to the trainmen on two-man cars.
4. When inaugurating one-man car service, it is good policy to assure the trainmen that no one will lose his job due to putting in the new cars. They are installed, as a rule, a line at a time, and experience has proved that the company is not burdened with extra men through this policy.
5. From the nature of the traffic available, the Safety Cars can accomplish more in a large city than in a small one, for the reason that the possibilities of increasing riding in the small community are limited. This statement is made to correct the erroneous impression existing in some minds that the Safety Car is useful only for saving expense in the smaller cities.
6. Where traffic is believed to be too heavy on peak to be successfully handled by Safety Cars, the larger, heavy cars may be used for tripper service on peak, thus making the light cars handle the long hour runs.
7. Similarly, where snow storms require the use of the heavier equipment at rare intervals, the Safety Cars can still be used to advantage during other times.
8. The Safety Car, though light, is just as substantial and with the same care in maintenance should last just as long as the former types of car. It has a steel frame and thoroughly modern, ventilated, interpole motors.
9. Regarding the matter of standardization, your Committee was not unanimous, but the majority opinion favored adhering to the present standard design of the Safety Car in the interest of cheaper costs through quantity production.
10. Experience has shown that the overwhelming majority of both riding public and trainmen favor the One-Man Safety Car; that it can, at one and the same time, improve the public's service, increase the trainman's wages and raise the company's profits; that it can be operated for about half the cost of an ordinary car; and that most of the companies that have tried it want more. We predict an increasingly rapid extension of the use of a device that can make a showing like the above.

General Features of the Safety Car

The standard Safety Car which is most commonly used is approximately 28 feet in length and seats 32 passengers, when arranged for double end operation. By utilizing the rear end, three additional seats can be obtained when the car is desired for single end operation only. The body is mounted on a single truck with 26 inch wheels and wheel base of about 8 feet. The construction of the truck is such that the car has excellent riding qualities and it is possible to use accelerating speeds, comparable to those of the competing automobile, without discomfort to passengers.

The Safety Car, completely equipped, weighs about 8 tons. It is of all steel construction and is built to a standard form and size. The roof is of the arch type and the sides are of steel with windows arranged for opening when desired. The platform is on the same plane as the body floor and folding doors and steps are equipped with mechanical opening and closing devices under control of the operator.

SAFETY CAR IN LEVIS, QUEBEC, EQUIPPED WITH GE-258 MOTORS AND K-63 CONTROLLERS

The electric equipment of the car consists of two 25-h.p. ventilated type railway motors, a type K-63 controller, special light weight grid resistors and a motor-driven air compressor, with a capacity of 10 cu. ft. per minute. Air brakes include various safety features and labor saving devices. The safety control equipment is especially adapted to the one-man operation; the brakes, doors, steps and sanders being controlled by a single brake handle and mutually interlocked.

As may be gathered from the above and from the following detailed description of air brakes and safety devices, the requirements of this type of car have been studied out with a great deal of care and to quote again from the report of the American Electric Railway Association, the development of this equipment has resulted in:

> "The creation of an entirely new type of car of low weight, greatly improved safety, and more rapid acceleration and deceleration. This car of the light weight safety type not only saves platform and accident expense, but permits an improvement in service, such as well nigh to revolutionize the street railway business."

MADISON RAILWAY COMPANY SAFETY CAR EQUIPPED WITH GE-258 MOTORS,
K CONTROL AND CP-25 COMPRESSORS

Improvement in Service

The effect of improved service by the use of Safety Cars is best shown by actual results in the following cities:

	% INCREASED SERVICE	% INCREASED GROSS RECEIPTS
Houston, Texas	80	60
El Paso, Texas	44	43
Tacoma, Washington	45	43
Seattle, Washington	55	67
Gary, Indiana	62	46
Terre Haute, Indiana	77	44
Tampa, Florida	51	51
Bridgeport, Connecticut	125	100

Power Consumption

Owing to the increased cost of power, due to the high price of coal, labor and materials, the reduction in energy consumption secured by the use of light weight Safety Cars is an important factor in their success. In some cases the adoption of this equipment has actually postponed indefinitely the purchase of additional

SAFETY CAR AT KEOKUK, IOWA, EQUIPPED WITH GE-258 MOTORS

power equipment. The power consumption is, of course, dependent upon the weight of the car, the number and duration of stops, speed, profile of the line, etc. It is, therefore, difficult to make any definite statement as to the actual power consumed except for a specific case, but it is evident that a car weighing 8 tons with two motors should operate with an energy consumption of approximately one-third that of a 24-ton car equipment with four motors. The average consumption on most city railway systems is approximately 3 kilowatt-hours per car mile. According to the A. E. R. A. report, the actual figures from forty-five companies show energy consumption of Safety Cars ranging from .8 to 1.75 kilowatt-hours per car mile.

Safety Car Installations

The total number of light weight Safety Cars in operation and on order in the United States at the present time is approximately 3600, not including rebuilt cars, many of which have been equipped with safety features and operated by one man. In general, the rebuilt cars have been used only on lines of light traffic, and their general use is not recommended.

The following tabulation shows the location, number of cars and names of operating companies, using light weight Safety Cars equipped with G-E motors and control:

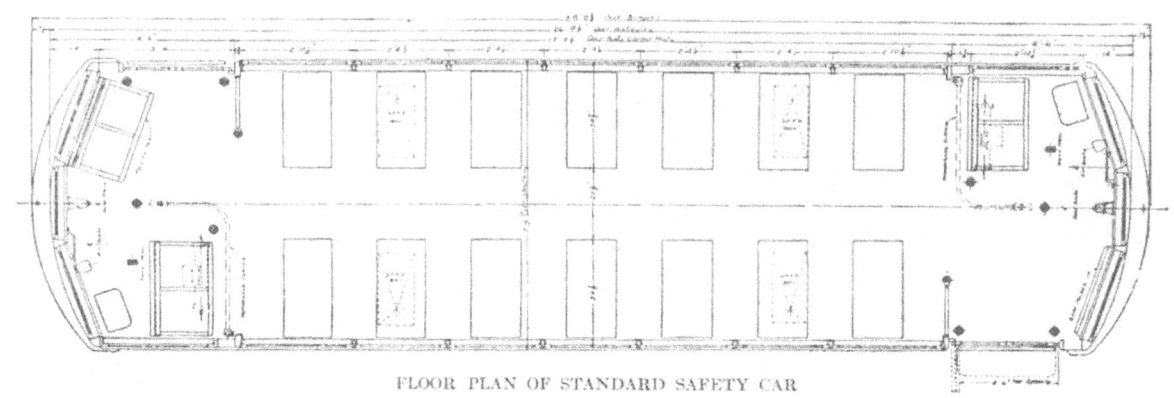

FLOOR PLAN OF STANDARD SAFETY CAR

By taking the results of many investigations as a basis it is possible to make a study of the financial results of replacing the ordinary types of heavy rolling stock using present day costs of operation, and thus secure a fairly accurate idea of what return can be counted upon for an investment made in Safety Cars. All such studies so far made, confirmed by actual results in every existing installation, indicate that the majority of roads cannot well neglect placing some of these cars in their service.

For instance, there are thousands of standard city cars which weigh about 40,000 lbs. and seat an average of 40 passengers. The Safety Car weighs 16,000 lbs. and seats 32 passengers. Its motive power consumption is approximately 50 per cent that of the heavier car. Its maintenance will be about 40% less. In many instances, where the cars replaced are exceptionally old or obsolete, the saving on maintenance will be much greater. The power ratio shown above has been repeatedly checked and verified; and the maintenance records of the earliest installations indicate the ratio shown is accurate after the cars have been in service from two to three years.

We show below the saving in equipment, maintenance and power which can be secured by the use of Safety Cars.

POWER AND MAINTENANCE CHARGES—CENTS PER CAR MILE

	40,000 LB. CAR	16,000 LB. CAR
Equipment maintenance	3.5	2
Power	4.2	2
Total	7.7	4

A car operating 18 hours daily on an 8.5 m.p.h. schedule which is the average for city service in practically all parts of the country will run approximately 56,000 miles a year. The heavy car costs for power and maintenance when making this mileage $4,312; the Safety Car $2,240; a saving of $2,072.

Platform expense for a two-man car averages 14.1 cents per car mile. An all-day car, including a 5% allowance for reporting and lay-up time, will run approximately 58,800 hours per year, costing in wages $8,280.

It has been customary to pay the operator of a one-man car a higher wage than either member of a two-man car. The average platform expense for a safety car is 7.75 cents per car mile. At this rate the platform expense for the safety car operators would be $4,554 annually or a saving of $3,726 as compared with a two-man car.

Car for car, therefore, the Safety Car on all day runs can save over $5,700 per year, and would pay for itself within 14 months. Car for car replacement is not recommended, as the best results are obtained by operating more cars on shorter headway, thus providing improved service. Experience has proved that most lines will stand at least 40% improvement in servie. This can best be accomplished by operating about 30% more cars and increasing the schedule speed 10%. For instance, instead of operating ten cars on a 10-minute headway, operate thirteen cars on a 7-minute headway, giving 8.5 cars per hour instead of six, a 40% increase. Reduced stops and higher accelerating and braking rates of the Safety Cars enable such a schedule speed increase to be easily made.

RUSH HOUR AT INDIANA STEEL COMPANY, GARY, IND. SAFETY CAR EQUIPPED WITH GE-258 MOTORS, K-63 CONTROL AND CP-25 COMPRESSORS

The costs and effect of such an increase can be shown as follows: assuming that only the regular all-day cars are replaced; using existing equipment for rush hour trippers.

The ten old cars running 8.5 m.p.h. make 560,000 car miles annually at a cost for power, maintenance and crew wages of $122,200.

Thirteen Safety Cars at 9.3 m.p.h. make 795,000 car miles per year; their cost for power and maintenance and crew wages will be $88,300; a saving of $33,900, while providing 40% more service.

The average receipts per car mile on street railways in the United States is 37.7 cents. The total receipts, therefore, for the ten old cars in this case will be $211,120. Experience shows that a 40% increase in service means approximately a 40% increase in receipts. Assuming only a 20% increase, this amounts to $42,200. The combined effect of reduced cost and increased gross is a net increase in earnings of $76,100 or approximately $7,600 per car annually for each heavy car displaced,

SAFETY CAR IN BUSINESS SECTION, GARY, IND.

which is equivalent to an annual return of 78% on the first cost of fifteen safety cars. This provides two spare cars. Taking increased fixed charges on the increased capital account, at 18% to cover interest, depreciation, taxes and insurance, there is still left a profit to the purchaser of better than 58% annually—enough to wipe out their cost in approximately two years.

Where traffic does not warrant increased service and the replacement is made car for car, 11 cars would probably be sufficient for a ten car line. The net savings would be approximately $58,000, equivalent to an annual return of approximately 80% of the first cost of eleven safety cars.

Probably in wide spread applications some lines would fall into one category, some into the other. An average result would unquestionably show, after paying all increased fixed charges including amortization, between $5,000 and $6,000 profit for each car displaced, a sum sufficient to pay the interest at 6% on $80,000 to $100,000 worth of securities.

The tabulated data following illustrates the economies and increased earning possibilities for each car displaced.

Column A—based on running equal mileage—no increase in cars.

Column B—based on running 40% more mileage with 30% more cars.

EASTERN MASSACHUSETTS ST. RY. SAFETY CAR EQUIPPED WITH GE-264 MOTORS, K-63 CONTROL

	Saving Made With	
	A EQUAL MILEAGE	B 40% INCREASE
Maintenance of equipment annual saving	$840.00	$370.00
Power	1,232.00	760.00
Crew wages	3,726.00	2,280.00
Total savings	$5,798.00	$3,410.00
Increased receipts at 20%		4,222.00
Increase in net earnings	$5,798.00	$7,632.00
Annual return on cost of safety car, approximately	80%	78%

The foregoing is based on average costs for labor and on the replacement of the heavier types of city cars. Average wage scales in many properties are materially lower and power consumption less. Many, moreover, will show lower average receipts per car mile. Under such conditions the savings of the Safety Car become less, but are still remarkable, as evidenced by the following figures representing about the lowest costs anywhere in the country today; they are the averages of representative roads operating in the smaller cities of the middle west and south. The average weight of the cars they operate is 30,000 lbs.; their average platform expense is 11.3 cents per car mile and their average receipts 30 cents per car mile.

Making a similar comparison to the one formerly shown, financial results would be as follows:

HOT SPRINGS ST. RY. SAFETY CAR EQUIPPED WITH GE-258 MOTORS, K-63 CONTROL AND CP-25 COMPRESSORS

OPERATING COSTS—CENTS PER CAR MILE

	30,000 LB. CAR	SAFETY CAR
Maintenance of equipment	2.5	1.5
Power	3.4	2
Total	5.9	3.5
Platform expense	11.3	6.23

SAVINGS AND EARNINGS—ALL DAY SERVICE

	EQUAL MILEAGE	40% INCREASE
Annual savings on maintenance	$560.00	$210.00
Annual savings on power	780.00	320.00
Annual savings on platform expense	2840.00	1870.00
Annual savings on total	$4180.00	$2400.00
Increased receipts at 20%		3360.00
Increased net earnings	$4180.00	$5760.00
Annual return on cost of safety car approximately	58%	63%

Even under these circumstances, the new cars would pay for themselves in less than two years; or if from these increased earnings be deducted interest, depreciation, taxes and insurance, there remains a clean profit of from $3,500 to $5,000 for each car displaced.

GE-258 MOTOR GE-264 MOTOR

G-E EQUIPMENT

The equipment developed by the General Electric Company, for the Safety Car, includes two 25-h.p. railway motors, a light weight platform type controller adapted for use with standard safety features, special light weight grid resistor, modified straight air brake equipment, also suitable for use with safety devices, and a ten-foot air compressor for supplying the air brake and accessory requirements.

MOTOR EQUIPMENT

The G-E 258 and G-E 264 motors have been most generally adapted for use on safety cars. They were designed for this service and are, for their capacity, the lightest weight railway motors manufactured. The G-E 258 has ball bearings on the armature shaft and weighs approximately 885 pounds. The G-E 264 has sleeve bearings of liberal design and weighs approximately 1000 lbs. The continuous capacity of these machines is so great that they operate at unusually low temperatures, and their performance, during the past five years, has been extremely satisfactory. These motors are fully described in Bulletins 44417A and 44470.

CONTROLLER

The K-63 controller was designed for use on light weight cars, is compact, occupies a minimum of platform space and weighs only 135 lbs. The controller is fully described in Bulletin 44678.

AIR BRAKE AND SAFETY FEATURES

The air brakes with safety features and labor saving devices are of special importance when the responsibility for the operation of a car is placed in the hands of one man instead of the usual crew of two. In the design of this equipment, every effort has been made to guard against accidents that might be caused by the disability or the inattention of the operator.

This equipment is a modification of the well known straight air brake with emergency features and safety devices which provide for bringing the car to a standstill automatically, should the operator by reason of sudden physical or mental disability

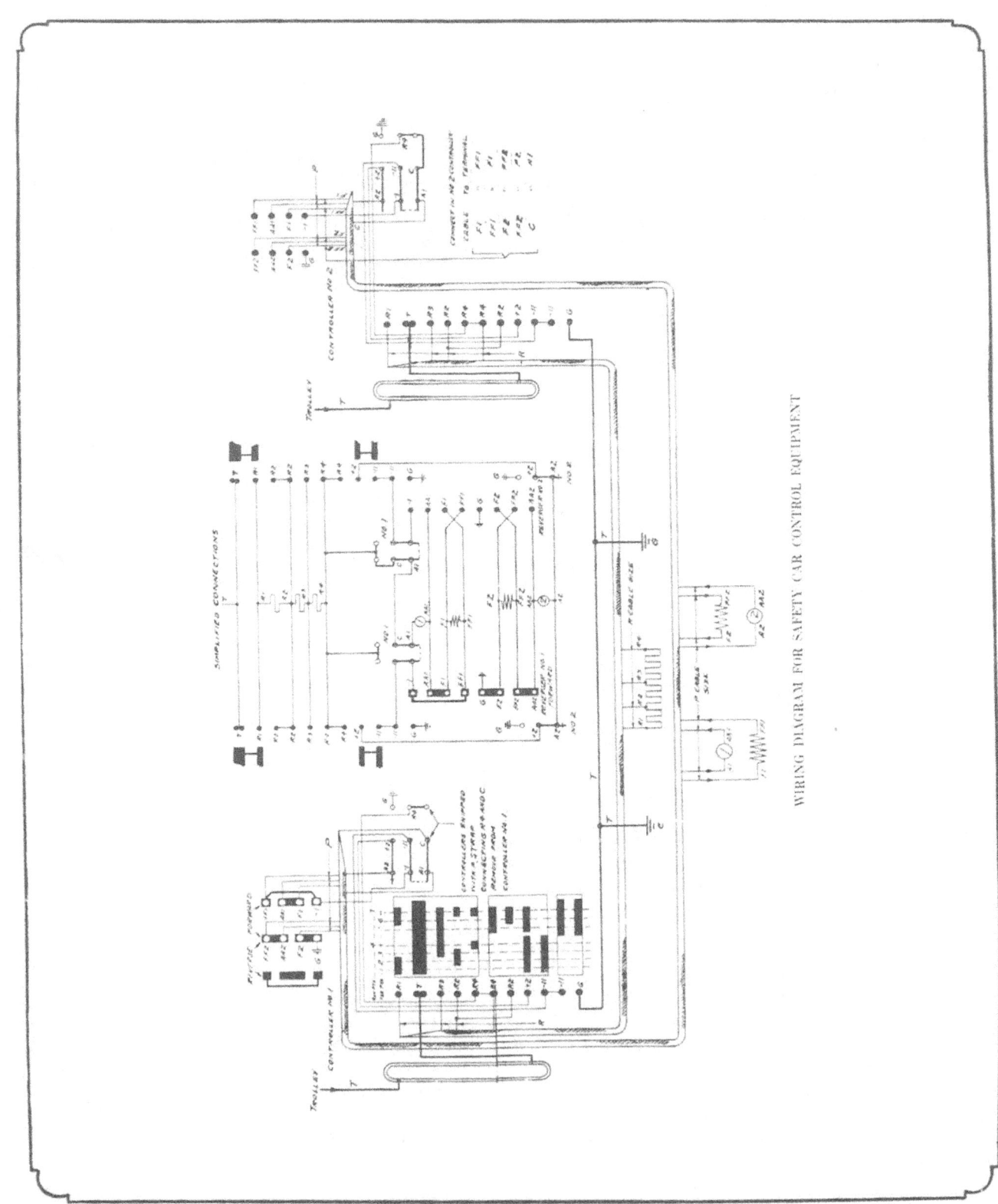

be unable to properly perform his duties. Normally, the brakes, doors, steps and sanders are controlled by the operator by means of a single brake valve, making it unnecessary for him to remove his hand from the brake valve handle to open the doors after the car has been brought to a stop, to close them when he is ready to proceed, or to manipulate the automatic sander. The brake valve is so constructed that a downward pressure on the handle in any of the several positions will cause sand to be applied to the rails.

The safety controller handle, which is an important part of this equipment, is so interlocked pneumatically with the brakes, doors, steps, sanders and a circuit-breaker tripping device, as to cause the brakes to apply automatically with full force if the operator removes his hand from it without having first made a brake application. In addition the circuit breaker is opened, sand is applied to the rail and doors are balanced so that they may be opened manually, if desired.

To relieve the operator of the necessity of keeping his hand on the controller handle at all times while the car is in motion, a relief valve known as the combined foot and cut-off valve is provided. This valve is installed in the safety control pipe and is located on the platform in such a position that the operator can reach it with his right foot. By holding this valve closed, the "dead-man's" feature is transferred from the controller handle to the foot valve. The latter is automatically held closed when a brake application of sufficient force to insure bringing the car to a stop has been made.

It is impossible for the brakes to "leak" off through carelessness on the part of the operator in leaving the car with the brake valve handle in "lap" position by reason of the fact that the combined foot and cut-off valve will automatically open if the brake cylinder pressure falls below a safe minimum. The opening of the foot valve under these conditions will result in emergency operation under which the brakes are applied with full force and maintained against leakage.

An emergency valve, which is located inside the car, automatically controls the brakes, door engines, sanders and circuit breaker cylinders under emergency conditions. This valve is actuated by a sudden reduction in pressure in either the safety control pipe

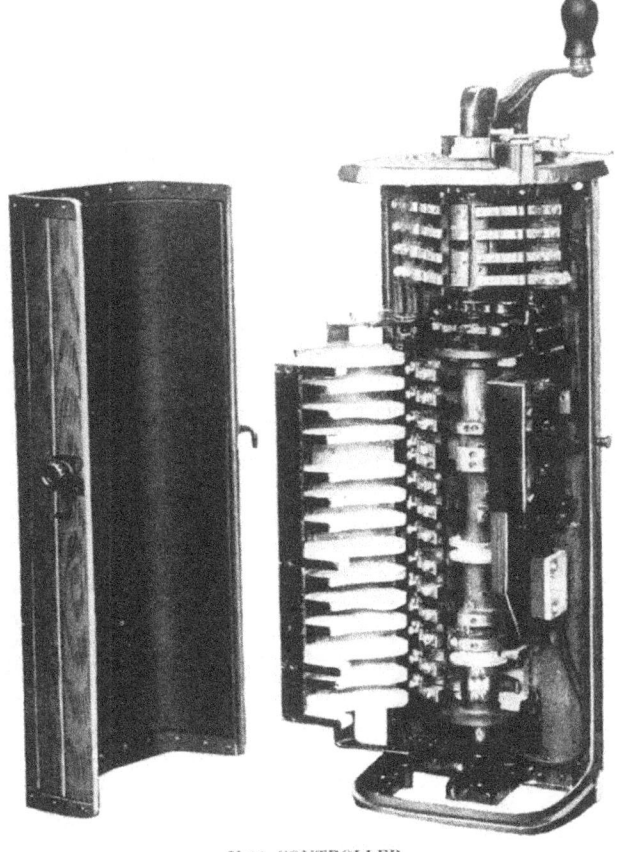

K-63 CONTROLLER

or emergency pipe, hence it will operate (1) if the operator removes his hand from the controller handle (or his foot from the foot valve) when the brakes are not applied; (2) if the operator moves the brake valve handle to emergency position; or, (3) if the pipe on either end of the car is accidentally broken or ruptured.

In all positions of the brake valve, except the door opening position, the door closing pipe is connected to the emergency line, hence when emergency operation takes place from any causes, pressure is automatically removed from the closing side of the door engines which permits of the doors being opened manually.

In the normal position of the emergency valve the sander reservoir is connected to the main reservoir thus keeping the former fully charged. When the emergency valve operates the sander reservoir is connected to the sanders and sand is blown onto the rail until the pressure in the sander reservoir is exhausted. This arrangement limits the time of automatic sanding in emergency and thus avoids an undue waste of sand.

Motor Driven Air Compressor

As compressed air is used for operating the brakes and all of the safety devices, it is imperative that the air compressor be of such design and construction as to insure continuity of servi e. The General Electric center gear type air compressor is in successful operation on approximately 1000 safety cars in all parts of the country and has fully demonstrated its many superior qualities in this class of service where schedule speeds are high and the demand for air is greater than heretofore.

These machines have duplex cylinders fitted with single acting trunk type pistons, and are driven through herring bone gearing by series wound motors having four salient poles.

For the standard safety car, we recommend the CP-25 (10 cu. ft.) compressor which, unless otherwise specified, is regularly furnished with equipments of this type. If desired, the next larger size compressor, the CP-27, which has a piston displacement of 15 cu. ft of free air per minute, will be furnished. A complete description and data on CP-25 and CP-27 compressors are given in Bulletin No. 44591A.

CONTROLLER HANDLE WITH
BASE AND PILOT VALVE
FOR SAFETY CAR
CONTROL.

EMERGENCY VALVE FOR AIR
BRAKE AND SAFETY CAR
CONTROL EQUIPMENT

BRAKE VALVE WITH SANDING FEATURE

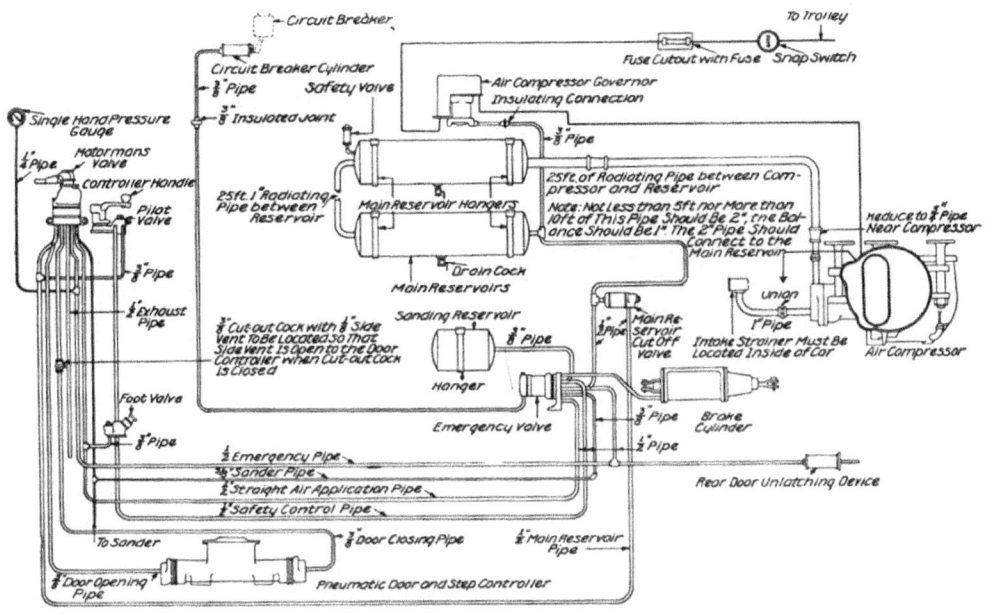

DIAGRAM OF AIR BRAKE AND SAFETY CAR CONTROL EQUIPMENT
FOR SINGLE END OPERATION

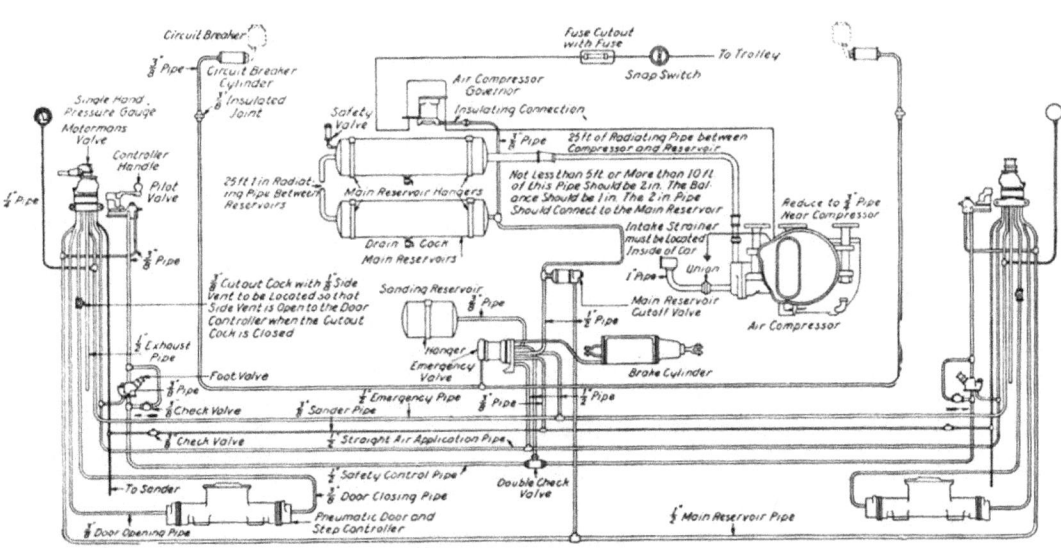

DIAGRAM OF AIR BRAKE AND SAFETY CAR CONTROL EQUIPMENT
FOR DOUBLE END OPERATION

CP-25 AIR COMPRESSOR   AIR COMPRESSOR GOVERNOR

Air Compressor Governor

The functions of the air compressor governor are to automatically start and stop the air compressor so as to maintain air pressure in the main reservoir within predetermined maximum and minimum limits. The air compressor governors manufactured by the General Electric Company were developed after a careful study of the rigid requirements of electric railway service, and are in successful use on thousands of cars throughout the country.

This type of governor is essentially a single-pole switch of the contactor type operated by means of a rubber diaphragm, a piston and a set of levers. The interrupting switch is provided with an arc chute of highly refractory material, an effective magnetic blowout and easily renewable contacts. The principle bearings are provided with hardened knife edges to reduce friction to a minimum, and to insure a quick snap action. Governors of this type are fully described in bulletin No. 44590.

Sioux City Service Co. 1947

SAFETY CARS WITH GENERAL ELECTRIC EQUIPMENT

RAILWAY	LOCATION	NO. OF CARS
ALABAMA		
Alabama Pr. Co.	Huntsville	2
Mobile Lt. & R.R. Co.	Mobile	10
ARKANSAS		
Fort Smith Lt. & Tr. Co.	Fort Smith	8
Hot Springs St. Ry. Co.	Hot Springs	7
Southwestern Gas & Elec. Co.	Texarkana	4
CALIFORNIA		
Los Angeles Ry. Corp.	Los Angeles	22
Pacific Elec. Ry. Co.	Las Angeles	13
Pacific Gas & Elec. Co.	Sacramento	6
Sacramento Northern R. R.	Oakland	2
San Francisco, Oakland Terminal Ry. Co.	San Diego	12
San Diego El Ry. Co.	Los Angeles and other properties	13
Southern Pacific R. R.		64
Stockton Elec. R. R. Co.	Stockton	5
COLORADO		
Colorado Springs & Int. Ry.	Colorado Springs	35
Denver & So. Platte Ry Co.	Denver	2
CONNECTICUT		
Bristol & Plainville Tramways Co.	Bristol	1
Connecticut Co.	Bridgeport, New Haven & Hartford	80
Danbury & Bethel St. Ry. Co	Danbury	7
FLORIDA		
Tampa Elec. Co.	Tampa	14
GEORGIA		
Columbus R. R. Co.	Columbus	17
Athens St. Ry.	Athens	6
ILLINOIS		
Aurora, Elgin & Chicago Ry.	Aurora	40
Central Ill. Public Serv. Co.	Mattoon	10
Centralia & Central City Traction	Centralia	4
Chicago, North Shore & Milwaukee R.R.	Waukegan	10
Illinois Northern Utilities Co.	Freeport	3
Illinois Trac System	Peoria, Quincy, Decatur, Galesburg, Wichita, Kansas and other properties	113
No. Kankakee El. Lt. & Ry. Co.	Kankakee	3
Pekin Municipal Ry.	Pekin	4
INDIANA		
Chic. So. Bend & Northern Ind. Ry. Co.	So. Bend	10
Fort Wayne & Northern Ind. Traction Co.	Fort Wayne	65
Gary & Hobart Tract. Co.	Gary	10
Gary & Hobart Tract. Co.	Hobart	1
Indiana Rys. & Lt. Co.	Kokomo	10
Louisville & South. Ind. Tract.	New Albany	
Terre Haute Trac. & Lt. Co.	Terre Haute	65
Washington St. Ry. Co.	Washington	3

RAILWAY	LOCATION	NO. OF CARS
IOWA		
Cedar Rapids & Marion City Ry.	Cedar Rapids	8
Keokuk Elec. Co.	Keokuk	3
Mason City & Clear Lake R.R.	Mason City	2
Ottumwa Ry. & Lt. Co.	Ottumwa	16
KANSAS		
Arkansas Valley Int. Ry. Co.	Newton	1
KENTUCKY		
Owensboro City R. R. Co.	Owensboro	10
LOUISIANA		
Baton Rouge Elec. Co.	Baton Rouge	8
New Orleans Ry. & Lt. Co.	New Orleans	40
MAINE		
Bangor Ry. & Elec. Co.	Bangor	15
Biddeford & Saco R. R. Co.	Biddeford	8
Lewiston, Augusta & Waterville St. Ry.	Lewiston	12
Cumberland County Pr. & Lt. Co.	Portland	21
MARYLAND		
United Ry. & Elec. Co.	Baltimore	23
MASSACHUSETTS		
Berkshire St. Ry. Co.	Pittsfield	17
Boston Elev. Ry. Co.	Boston	31
Brockton & Plymouth St. Ry.	Plymouth	2
Eastern Mass. St. Ry.	Boston	101
Worcester Const. St. Ry.	Worcester	19
MICHIGAN		
Benton Harbor & St. Joe Ry. & Lt. Co.	Benton Harbor	2
Grand Rapids Ry. Co.	Grand Rapids	19
Ironwood & Bessemer Ry. & Lt. Co.	Ironwood	3
Michigan Ry. Co.	Jackson	20
Michigan Ry. Co.	Kalamazoo	16
Saginaw, Bay City Ry.	Saginaw	26
MINNESOTA		
Duluth St. Ry.	Duluth	6
St. Cloud Public Serv. Co.	St. Cloud	2
Wisconsin Ry. Lt. & Pr. Co.	Winona	38
MISSISSIPPI		
Vicksburg Lt. & Trac. Co.	Vicksburg	2
MISSOURI		
City Lt. & Tr. Co.	Sedalia	8
Kansas City Rys.	Kansas City	29
St. Joseph Ry. Lt. & P. Co.	St. Joseph	12
St. Louis Water Works Ry.	St. Louis	2
Union Depot Bridge & Ter. Co.	Kansas City	8
NEBRASKA		
Lincoln Traction Co.	Lincoln	32
Omaha & Council Bluffs St. Ry. Co.	Omaha	5
Omaha, Lincoln & Beatrice Ry. Co.	Lincoln	1

RAILWAY	LOCATION	NO. OF CARS
NEW HAMPSHIRE		
Laconia St. Ry.	Laconia	4
Nashua St. Ry.	Nashua	8
NEW JERSEY		
Trenton & Mercer County Trac. Co.	Trenton	62
Morris County Tract. Co.	Morristown	14
Penn. & New Jersey Ry. Co.	Trenton	13
NEW YORK		
Brooklyn Rapid Transit Co.	Brooklyn	106
Elmira Water Lt. & R. R. Co.	Elmira	7
Geneva, Seneca Falls & Auburn R. R. Co.	Seneca Falls	2
New York & Stamford Ry. Co.	Port Chester	7
Westchester St. R. R. Co.	White Plains	6
NORTH CAROLINA		
Carolina Pr. & Lt. Co.	Raleigh	19
North Carolina Public Serv. Co.	Greensboro	4
Southern Public Utilities Co.	Charlotte	21
NORTH DAKOTA		
Grand Forks St. Ry. Co.	Grand Forks	6
OHIO		
Northern Ohio Tr. & Lt. Co.	Akron	25
Richland Public Serv. Co.	Mansfield	7
Ohio Service Co.	Coshocton	2
OKLAHOMA		
Oklahoma Union Ry.	Tulsa	18
Pittsburgh County Ry.	McAlester	6
OREGON		
Portland Ry. Lt. & Pr. Co.	Portland	25
PENNSYLVANIA		
Mahoning & Shenango Ry. & Lt. Co.	New Castle & Sharon	18
Conestoga Traction Co.	Lancaster	4
Northumberland County Ry. Co.	Sunbury	4
Eastern Penn. Ry.	Pottsville	10
Northwestern Penn. Ry.	Meadville	6
Reading Transit & Lt. Co.	Reading	12
Trenton, Bristol & Phila. St. Ry.	Bristol	6
RHODE ISLAND		
Newport & Providence Ry.	Newport	3
SOUTH DAKOTA		
Aberdeen R. R. Co.	Aberdeen	8
TEXAS		
Austin St. Ry.	Austin	20
Dallas St. Ry. Co.	Dallas	12
Eastern Texas Elec. Co.	Beaumont	13
El Paso Elec. Co.	El Paso	30
Houston Elec. Co.	Houston	39
Marshall Traction Co.	Marshall	2
Northern Texas Tract. Co.	Fort Worth	75
Texas Elec. Ry.	Waco	16
Wichita Falls Tr. Co.	Wichita Falls	4
VERMONT		
Rutland Ry. Lt. & Pr. Co.	Rutland	1
VIRGINIA		
Virginia Ry. & Pr. Co.	Richmond & Norfolk	40
WASHINGTON		
North Coast Pr. Co.	Vancouver	2
Puget Sound Tr. Lt. & Pr. Co.	Seattle, Everett, Tacoma, Bellingham	83
WEST VIRGINIA		
Charleston-Dunbar Tr. Co.	Charleston	4
WISCONSIN		
Beloit Trac. Co.	Beloit	4
Eastern Wisconsin Elec. Co.	Sheboygan	15
Eastern Wis. El. Co.	Oshkosh	13
Madison Rys. Co.	Madison	13
Milwaukee El. Ry & Lt. Co.	Racine	40
Wisconsin Ry. Lt. & Pr. Co.	La Crosse	8
Wisconsin Valley El Co.	Wausau	3
CANADA		
Cape Breton Elec. Co., Ltd.	Sydney, N. S.	2
Levis County Ry.	Levis, Quebec	12
Nova Scotia Tramway & Pr. Co.	Halifax, N. S.	24
Peterboro Radial Ry.	Peterboro, Ont.	2
CUBA		
Matanzas Elec. St. Ry.	Matanzas	15
MEXICO		
Mexico Tramways Co.	Mexico City	6

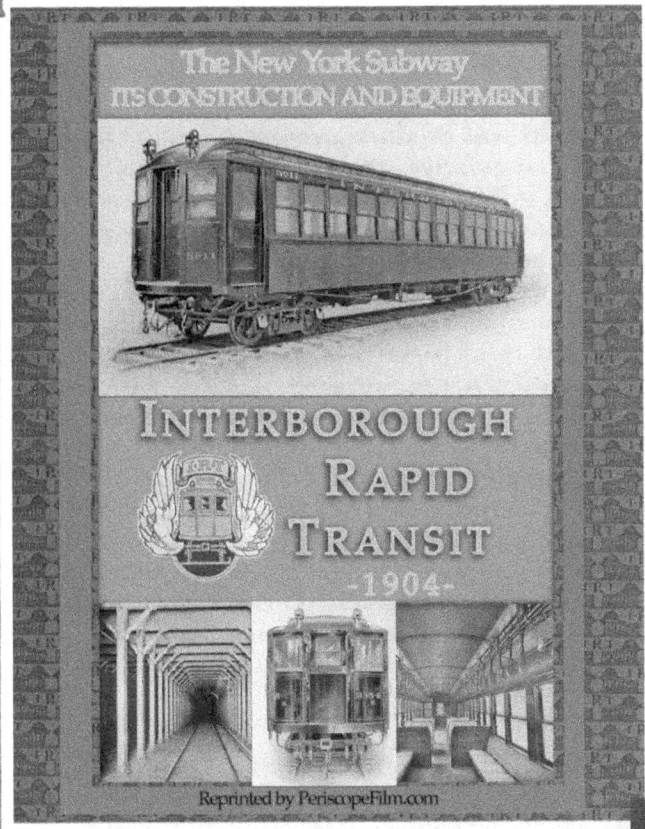

On October 27, 1904, the Interborough Rapid Transit Company opened the first subway in New York City. Running between City Hall and 145th Street at Broadway, the line was greeted with enthusiasm and, in some circles, trepidation. Created under the supervision of Chief Engineer S.L.F. Deyo, the arrival of the IRT foreshadowed the end of the "elevated" transit era on the island of Manhattan. The subway proved such a success that the IRT Co. soon achieved a monopoly on New York public transit. In 1940 the IRT and its rival the BMT were taken over by the City of New York. Today, the IRT subway lines still exist, primarily in Manhattan where they are operated as the "A Division" of the subway. Reprinted here is a special book created by the IRT, recounting the design and construction of the fledgling subway system. Originally created in 1904, it presents the IRT story with a flourish, and with numerous fascinating illustrations and rare photographs.

Originally written in the late 1900's and then periodically revised, A History of the Baldwin Locomotive Works chronicles the origins and growth of one of America's greatest industrial-era corporations. Founded in the early 1830's by Philadelphia jeweler Matthais Baldwin, the company built a huge number of steam locomotives before ceasing production in 1949. These included the 4-4-0 American type, 2-8-2 Mikado and 2-8-0 Consolidation. Hit hard by the loss of the steam engine market, Baldwin soldiered on for a brief while, producing electric and diesel engines. General Electric's dominance of the market proved too much, and Baldwin finally closed its doors in 1956. By that time over 70,500 Baldwin locomotives had been produced. This high quality reprint of the official company history dates from 1920. The book has been slightly reformatted, but care has been taken to preserve the integrity of the text.

NOW AVAILABLE AT
WWW.PERISCOPEFILM.COM

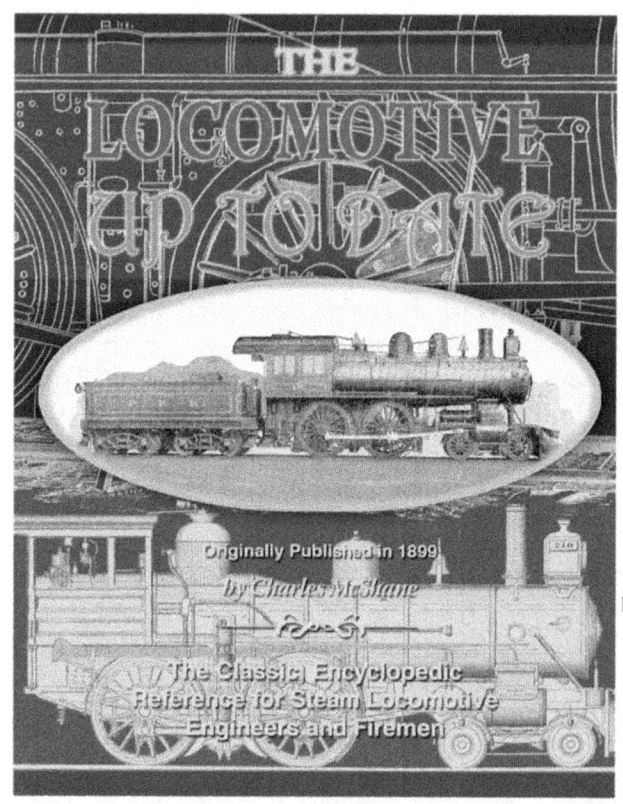

When it was originally published in 1899, **The Locomotive Up to Date** was hailed as "...the most definitive work ever published concerning the mechanism that has transformed the American nation: the steam locomotive." Filled with over 700 pages of text, diagrams and photos, this remains one of the most important railroading books ever written. From steam valves to sanders, trucks to side rods, it's a treasure trove of information, explaining in easy-to-understand language how the most sophisticated machines of the 19th Century were operated and maintained. This new edition is an exact duplicate of the original. Reformatted as an easy-to-read 8.5x11 volume, it's delightful for railroad enthusiasts of all ages.

Originally printed in 1898 and then periodically revised, **The Motorman...and His Duties** served as the definitive training text for a generation of streetcar operators. A must-have for the trolley or train enthusiast, it is also an important source of information for museum staff and docents. Lavishly illustrated with numerous photos and black and white line drawings, this affordable reprint contains all of the original text. Includes chapters on trolley car types and equipment, troubleshooting, brakes, controllers, electricity and principles, electric traction, multi-car control and has a convenient glossary in the back. If you've ever operated a trolley car, or just had an electric train set, this is a terrific book for your shelf!

ALSO NOW AVAILABLE FROM PERISCOPEFILM.COM!

THE CLASSIC 1911 TROLLEY CAR BUILDER'S REFERENCE BOOK

ELECTRIC RAILWAY DICTIONARY

By Rodney Hitt
Associate Editor, Electric Railway Journal

REPRINTED BY PERISCOPEFILM.COM

©2010 Periscope Film LLC
All Rights Reserved
ISBN #978-1-935700-22-7
www.PeriscopeFilm.com

www.ingramcontent.com/pod-product-compliance
Lightning Source LLC
LaVergne TN
LVHW061347060426
835512LV00012B/2593